HAUNTED
MONTEREY
COUNTY

HAUNTED MONTEREY COUNTY

PATRICK WHITEHURST

FEATURING ILLUSTRATIONS FROM PAUL VAN DE CARR

Haunted
America

Published by Haunted America
A Division of The History Press
Charleston, SC
www.historypress.com

Cover image: The Carmel Mission is one of the most visited landmarks in Monterey County and rumored to be one of the most haunted. *Author's collection.*

First published 2019

Manufactured in the United States

ISBN 9781467142359

Library of Congress Control Number: 2019943522

For Randall A. Reinstedt, one of the nicest guys—not to mention one of the Central Coast's best writers.

CONTENTS

CONTENTS

ACKNOWLEDGEMENTS

They say people make the world go 'round. People also make *books* go 'round. Were it not for the energy of the people of the Monterey Peninsula, this book would never have made it to print. By "energy," I'm talking about their eyeballs on the pages, their gray matter switched into editorial mode, their memories powered backward in time like the DeLorean in the *Back to the Future* movies. Randall A. Reinstedt, to whom this book is dedicated, and his wife, Debbie, were of invaluable assistance. Thanks also to Paul Van de Carr for his amazing creative work in designing the art for this book. A big hug to Natalia Molina for her patience and for not sighing every time I asked her opinion on something…but also for getting scared on our investigative outings. It made it more fun. I would also like to thank Laurie Krill, with Arcadia Publishing and The History Press, for her help in getting this book to print. She was an invaluable part of the process. Thank you. Thanks also to the folks with the California State Parks, Nikki Guichet, Kate Roberts, everyone at the Steinbeck House, the folks at Stevenson House, the helpful folks at the Carmel Mission, those great students at Salinas High School and to so many others who offered their stories. Your contributions added just the right amount of chill.

PROLOGUE

You're going to die.

I'm going to die. It happens to the best of us—unless, of course, you believe the stories about Walt Disney, Tupac and Elvis. Rich or poor, we all punch out when our shift is up. Some of us, many believe, don't go all the way to that long goodnight, however. They die, sure, but they don't *leave*. This book takes a look at some of the locations on the California Central Coast, in gorgeous Monterey County, where the dead remain living. It could be they're only living because those of us still breathing air have breathed life into them through stories and eerie encounters that can't be explained.

When I was a kid in Seaside, California, my mother introduced me and my brother to local history by way of author Randall A. Reinstedt, who at the time was hard at work on his local tales of ghostly encounters. We had two of his books in the house. Besides my old *Kung Fu* comics, Reinstedt's creepy *Ghosts, Bandits & Legends of Old Monterey* was the most earmarked bit of reading material in the house. I pored over every passage, from the stories of spirits at the Carmel Mission to the woman in lace seen on 17-Mile Drive, and I begged my mom to take us in her 1970s Volkswagen Beetle to every spot depicted in the book, hoping that I, too, would become an eyewitness to something so strange my brain would have a tough time recuperating from the shock. Sadly, I never encountered anything more alarming than a tingle running up my spine.

It was these tales of local lore, however, that led me to gather my own collection of regional stories in the 1990s while living in Williams, Arizona. I wrote down every creepy tale I could find from the area. Later, when I became a journalist for the *Williams–Grand Canyon News*, I jumped at the chance to report on stories of the occult whenever and wherever they popped up. Like Monterey County, there are plenty of stories at the Gateway to the Grand Canyon. But my memories always fell back on those days and nights (hiding under the blankets) with Reinstedt's book in my hands. I was thrilled to see how many other stories he'd produced over the years when I returned to the Peninsula in 2014. I'm equally thrilled to make my own contribution to the Monterey Peninsula and jumped at the chance to explore parts of the area I grew up in through the eyes of an adult.

This book chronicles the chilling tales of supernatural phenomena from areas all over Monterey County. While Monterey itself may have the most traffic when it comes to spiritual phenomena, there are ghostly stories in the surrounding cities as well, from Big Sur to Salinas and beyond. We take a look at bleak tales of ghostly hauntings in old Fort Ord, visit the Steinbeck House in Salinas for a lunchtime ghostly encounter and wander through the heart of Monterey at some of the city's most haunted locations. Could the ghost of author John Steinbeck still roam the halls of his birth home? Could the death of his friend Ed Ricketts be on continuous paranormal repeat at the scene of his demise? Many believe that to be the case. In these pages, you'll learn more about the various cases and reports that have developed Monterey County into one of California's most haunted locales. The incidents shared here encompass a wide array of sources, including newspapers with their online links found in the bibliography, a number of books printed on the subject pertaining to the county and testimonies offered in person by the kind individuals working and living around these haunted locales. Many of the stories were shared first- and secondhand, with some expanding on the same tales found within the area's collection of ghost books and others sharing stories found on paranormal websites devoted to the topic and never before shared in print; still other accounts have never been told before now.

PART I
AROUND THE BAY

DRAMA IN THE CAPITAL

To say that Monterey County is rich with paranormal activity would be an understatement. Tales of the unknown zigzag the county, with the highest concentration found in the old capital itself: Monterey, California. There's no telling what makes this so, but as with other haunted locales across the globe, it has a lot to do with its story. The longer a place has been around, the more pages there are in its scrapbook.

Before Europeans ever laid eyes on the Central Coast, the land was inhabited by Native American tribes such as the Rumsien, Ohlone, Costanoan, Esselen and Salinan tribes. The area—surrounded by forest, temperate conditions year-round and easy access to the sea—made for easy hunting and fishing for the people who lived here. They inhabited the area for thousands of years prior to the arrival of the first European visitor in 1602. More than one hundred years passed before things really began to change for the tribes, however.

That change came in 1770, when Franciscan Father Junípero Serra, canonized as a saint by Pope Francis in 2015, arrived with Don Gaspar de Portolá's expedition and laid the groundwork for the first mission facing Monterey Bay itself in what is today known as Monterey's Presidio. It was a tired expedition that landed on the cool, foggy shores of the bay.

The path north from San Diego was reported fraught with hardship, and many celebrated the erection of the Holy Cross on the hill leading to shoreline. It was there they built the first mission in Monterey, but the structure was not destined to remain in that location. Due to conflicts between those who called the area home and members of the expedition, Father Serra chose to move the mission to Carmel, where it remains to this day.

Artist's rendering of dark riders gathered outside the Mission San Carlos Borromeo in Carmel, California. *Drawing by Paul Van de Carr.*

In 1776, Monterey was named the capital of California. Spanish colonists began to arrive that same year. Soon the city began to grow outward, despite a brief sacking by Argentinian revolutionaries. By 1818, streets and homes began to populate the area, and the layout of Monterey as it appears today began to take shape. California then joined with Mexico in 1822, after the country gained its independence from Spain. Monterey became the port of call for all international traders in the state. Many who visited the area first paid a call to the Custom House to attend to matters of commerce. The structure still stands to this day near Old Fisherman's Wharf, both of which will be explored in great detail as we continue. A consulate was established soon after due to a large influx of American visitors. Following a brief occupation by the American military, California was made a part of the United States in 1848 and gained statehood in 1850, which happened in the city of Monterey at Colton Hall. Around that time, the area's famed Chinese Fishing Village appeared on the shoreline of what is today known as Pacific Grove. There local fishing grew exponentially, leading to the eventual rise of Cannery Row and additions to the popular Fisherman's Wharf, which lasted until the 1970s.

The area's beauty quickly attracted visitors of a different type by the 1880s. Monterey soon became a hub for tourism, particularly following the expansion of the Hotel Del Monte. With railroad tracks for the Southern Pacific Rail line now laid through town, commerce moved to a whole new level on the Peninsula. World Wars I and II brought great demand to the canneries, ushering in a new wave of growth to the already booming canning industry. In 1945, author John Steinbeck made Cannery Row famous with his book of the same name, although not everyone in the community appreciated his depiction of life in Monterey. Although the canneries would eventually close, after causing decades of ecological damage to the bay itself, tourism continued on the coastal road along the city's shore. The Monterey Bay Aquarium opened in 1984 and, combined with the AT&T Pebble Beach Pro Am and other events, led to the Central Coast's current reputation as a premier destination for world travelers.

Others besides tourists were drawn to the area as well. Over the years, many authors would come to love and write about the Peninsula. Its most famous literary resident, John Steinbeck, was born in Salinas in 1902. Beat writer Jack Kerouac also visited town (and was quite fond of Big Sur), as did Hunter S. Thompson and other contemporary authors. Robert

Louis Stevenson lived in the area for a period (albeit brief), as did the poet Robinson Jeffers, who built the grand Tor House in Carmel. Their presence can still be felt along the shore and within the breezy pines of Monterey County—whether a result of ghostly sightings or through the streets and buildings named for them.

When it comes to paranormal activity, ghosts are widely believed to exist above all other types of mysterious phenomena, including near-death experiences and the ability to talk to the dead. Some take or leave aspects of the paranormal, but many believe in ghosts themselves. In many cultures, spirits are recognized and accommodated. Here in America, a 2013 Harris Poll found that 43 percent of the population believes in ghosts. Are ghosts merely disconnected memories doomed to play on repeat for all of eternity, or are they the embodiment of a person's soul that remains after death, seeking a way to cross to the other side? There is very little hard evidence on the existence of ghosts, but there are plenty of stories and unexplained occurrences, such as lights that act with a life of their own, strange sounds and foggy shapes caught on security video that seem to "walk" across a room. They range from violent poltergeists and shadow people to innocent spirits hanging out in the kitchen of your house.

Descriptions of ghosts have also fallen under a classification system, indicating to us the sort of spirit haunting a particular location. This includes mists, known as ectoplasm; poltergeists, which translates to "noisy ghosts" due to the fact that poltergeists are alleged to have the ability to move objects in the physical world; orbs, which some believe are the first state of transition before a spirit becomes a full-fledged ghost; and cold spots, which can signal the presence of a funnel ghost, a swirling burst of light or a haze. Funnel ghosts are usually attributed to a visit from a loved one.

One such phantasm, which a witness claimed in an online message board to have seen along the shore in Monterey, floated more than three feet in the air while wearing a flowing white dress and making gestures with her arm. According to the witness, no one saw the spirit but him—not even a dog that meandered along the shore right under the floating spirit's feet. This floating white form, with no discernable face, slowly retreated through the fog, back to what appeared to the witness to be the deck of an old ship, although it was hard to make out in the soupy air.

Another would be the playful spirit of Jack Swan, long rumored to haunt California's First Theatre in Monterey. Swan built the small adobe, near the Custom House, on the corner of Pacific and Scot Streets between 1846 and 1847. It's said that he built the structure using lumber harvested from an old shipwreck and used it as both a home and a tavern at first, before he added to the place. The building, while now closed to the public for the foreseeable future due to structural issues, went on to become a bustling tavern and lodge for sailors coming to shore from Monterey Bay. By 1850, the building had become a theater for stage productions put on by U.S. Army officers. Swan himself built the stage and the benches for seating, provided whale oil lamps and even made curtains for the shows, which cost $5 per ticket. It's thought to be the first theater in California to charge a fee for admission. On its opening night, historians with the California State Parks say, the theater brought in a whopping $500. Not bad for one curtain, especially in the 1800s. The theater eventually returned to being a lodging house for whalers, but its reputation as a theater never went away. Swan died in the late 1890s, and in 1906 the theater became the property of the California Historic Landmarks League, which in turn donated it to the State of California. It was then opened for theater shows once again.

While Swan may have died those many years ago, his love for the historic old building hasn't gone away. Born in 1817 as John Alfred Swan but going by the name of Jack, Swan himself was a sailor of Scottish ancestry who came to Monterey in 1843. As so many do who come to the Peninsula, he decided to call the place home. The theater, in fact, is often referred to as "the house that Jack built." And there are many who believe that the spirit of Jack Swan can still be felt in the old building.

Voices can often be heard calling down from the rafter overlooking the stage—strange, disembodied voices that startle those passing beneath and lead to the notion that the spirit is having a bit of lively fun with those in the land of the living. Others claim to have seen objects move within the building as if they had a mind of their own. More than anything, many have reported a feeling of being watched in the years since Swan passed. Jeff Dwyer, ghost hunter and author of the *Ghost Hunter's Guide to Monterey and the California Central Coast*, claimed to have seen Swan's ghost on more than one occasion.

Are these apparitions made up of electromagnetic fields, detectable with modern-day equipment such as microphones, infrared cameras and electromagnetic field (EMF) detectors? Or are they something more? In Monterey, ghost stories range from the yellow blob at Steinbeck's birth home in Salinas to riders on horseback at the Carmel Mission and uncanny cold zones on Cannery Row, where one of its most famous residents was hit by an oncoming train. These spirits are property owners who lived in the area, writers, children and even large groups of spirits clustered in a single location.

Monterey is where to find them.

THE CUSTOM HOUSE GHOSTS

When the fog lifted from the chilly Pacific Ocean, sailors knew that their destination was near. The outline of the mountainous Santa Lucia Range would come into view, and the warble of gulls sounded high overhead. The sea changed in subtle ways as boats crossed into Monterey Bay, and the braying of sea lions grew louder and louder.

It hadn't always been the case for the seafaring men of business. Spain once ruled the land and forbade international trade, but following Mexico's independence, California pledged allegiance to its southerly neighbors. Now a part of Mexico, the city enjoyed new prosperity under the country's open border policy, allowing these sailors the chance to open up new opportunities

A postcard depiction of the front porch of the Custom House as it looked in the early 1900s. *Detroit Publishing Company Collection.*

for commerce. During the nineteenth century, trade was the most important revenue source for the state, most of which occurred on the shore of Monterey Bay. It remained that way until about 1860, when San Francisco took over as the main port of entry for the state.

As part of the Mexican territory known as Alta California, Monterey Bay was an important port for seafaring crews before the late 1800s. It was a place where sailors could rest from a long sea voyage and earn a decent income by selling their wares, be that coffee, rice and sugar or other merchandise. As with all merchant vessels of foreign origin, the crew would first check in at the Custom House to pay their taxes to the Mexican government. The modest Spanish Colonial–style adobe is thought to have been built around the year 1827.

These weary sailors wouldn't have to walk far, as the site is mere steps from the shoreline; as it was part of the state's capital and the main port of call for many years, the soldiers might have had a long wait until an inspector could process their cargo and conclude their business.

Death was never far from the Custom House in those early days of its existence. Many have reported ghosts in the old adobe, with some of those apparitions thought to be sailors who perished there over the years. There is mention among local ghost researchers of a Mexican man and boy who were murdered inside the building. Theirs is a commonly known story among residents of Monterey. Their spirits are said to still inhabit the old building. The lingering spirit of an elderly man has also been reported at the site. Witnesses have reported hearing his ghostly voice and hearing him cough even when no other living souls were present. Other incidents include a ghostly black cat that is said to appear and disappear at will.

This may hail back to a time when the structure housed a rather large family, prior to 1929 and before it became a state landmark, long after sailors stopped selling their wares through Monterey. The building had fallen to ruin and no longer served as a charming welcome to sailors from around the world, although its dilapidated state didn't stop the poor family from making a home there. Many of the stories relate to one particular side of the building, near the stairwell that led to the building's tower. The family, according to local ghost historian Randall A. Reinstedt, reported multiple visits from the ghosts of the murdered man and boy. The family first saw the spirits in the dead of night, when the older of the two spirits told the tale of their deaths. The man and his young companion, whose ghostly image stood close by, were killed for the

The Custom House in Monterey as it appears today. The structure has been a part of the Monterey landscape since the 1820s. *Author's collection.*

gold they had hidden somewhere in the old adobe building. He told the family that their bodies had been buried at the foot of the stairs leading to one of the structure's two towers. They pleaded with the family to locate their bones. This cursed wraith yearned for one thing only, something so many others are gifted with when they die: a decent burial. For the man and boy, they requested a Catholic burial. Try as they might, however, the family could not locate the bones anywhere. Without a resolution to their predicament, the spirits continued to visit the family. These spirits, being particularly persistent, even appeared as skeletons at one point, according to Reinstedt.

The idea of hidden gold coins proved too enticing for the family. According to the story, they searched in vain for the treasure the spirits said was hidden there, prying up the floors and searching every inch of the corner of the house the ghost indicated. No gold, and no corpses, was ever found. The spirits reportedly grew so troubled that they threw the man of the house from his bed while he was sleeping—not once but *three* times during the course of a single evening—leading to the family's ultimate decision to abandon the search and move to a new home.

Since these events, the Custom House has remained largely the same. This is by design, as the building is now a tourist destination and the first state landmark, according to the California Department of Parks and Recreation. As the oldest government building in the state, the department now offers tours of Custom House Plaza to approximate the experience of early traders when they visited the building in the 1800s. A gift shop is also located on the premises.

Current docents and park officials, many of whom have worked at the Custom House for more than a decade, said they've not seen or heard anything supernatural while working there. Could the ghosts have found the rest they sought after so many years of turmoil? Or are they merely biding their time, waiting for the right opportunity to see an end to their immortal existence?

Located within a stone's throw of the Custom House is Old Fisherman's Wharf, one of the most visited sites for those spending their vacation in Monterey County. The wharf was built in 1845 by Thomas Larkin to accommodate ships coming into the bay, which came to port four times weekly bearing both passengers and freight. The City of Monterey took ownership of the wharf in 1913. By this time, the sardine industry was booming in town thanks to the plentiful harvest found swimming in its front yard.

The wharf continued to grow in the 1920s. By this time, the structure featured a marine science station, a secondary "finger" pier, wholesale and retail fish outlets, restaurants and warehouses for storage of the prized products fished from the sea. To meet the ever-growing demand for this product, however, more space was required. This led to the construction in 1925 of the cargo wharf, designed to allow room for the bulging commercial fishing fleet and lighten congestion on Fisherman's Wharf—the "Old" part of its name not being added until later, of course. Four years later, funds were approved for the creation of a breakwater as well, which today features more sea lions than it does people. Commercial fishing remained the primary wharf business until after World War II. In the 1950s, the wharf began to cater to tourists more than businesses. Snack shops, an aquarium, boat rentals, a theater and gift shops began to pop up, while the commercial wharf nearby catered to the fishing fleets.

Today, the wharf is known for its whale watching tours, fine restaurants, views of sea otters and other marine life and even as a filming location for television and films. The popular spot was featured in the HBO series *Big Little Lies* in its first season. The series stars Nicole Kidman, Reese Witherspoon, Shailene Woodley and more.

While there aren't many ghostly tales concerning the wharf, there are just enough stories to pique the interest of any budding paranormal investigator. These coastal hauntings typically occur late at night on the commercial pier, where many of the restaurants and shops can be found. On any given evening, late into the night when the shops have closed and tourists have snuggled safely in their beds, a foul odor is said to creep over the wharf, saturating the shops and street with the stench of dried kelp and dead fish. That smell, some say, precedes the appearance of mysterious spirits. Often the spirits have been seen on benches staring out to sea before they disappear and are typically dressed in galoshes, fishing or sailor attire. Some of these spirits have even spoken when approached, according to eyewitness accounts, although no one has been able to readily identify who the spirits are.

A short walk from both locations, one finds yet another haunted adobe. This one was built later than some of Monterey's older structures, however. The Old Whaling Station was built around the same time as the wharf by Englishman David Wight. Originally intended as a home for his family—designed, in fact, to look something like his ancestral home in Scotland—the Wight House would not remain a family home for long, however. When the gold rush hit, Wight packed up his family and headed for the Sierra Mountains to strike it rich. The home was sold to a new owner, and a second balcony was installed in the early 1900s. By this time, the Wight House had been leased to the Old Monterey Whaling Company. It intended to use the property as the headquarters for its newly formed company, as it faced the Monterey Bay perfectly. The company, made up primarily of Portuguese fishermen, according to Reinstedt, was the first whaling company established on the shores of Monterey. Like many of the other historic buildings around Monterey, the Old Whaling Station Adobe is now owned by the State of California.

It's here in the Old Whaling Station Adobe, formerly the Wight House, where cold spots have been reported over the years, as well as a feeling that chills you to the bone in certain sections of the home, particularly upstairs. One occasion, a security guard even recounted that the curtains in the room billowed outward as if an invisible person were passing through them. Years later, one person was also reportedly shoved from behind, but when he turned to investigate who had pushed him, there was no one there. On another occasion, an old fisherman was spotted in the backyard of the property by police during their late-night rounds. When the fisherman refused their summons, the officers gave chase and tried to tackle the man. When they got up after the tackle, they found there was no one there. These are only a few of the stories surrounding the old building, but they paint a strong picture of what is another entry in Monterey's vast catalogue of haunted spots.

TYPHOID FEVER AT THE STEVENSON HOUSE

The Stevenson House is neatly tucked away on Houston Street in the heart of downtown Monterey—so neatly, in fact, that it can be easy to pass by without seeing it! The historic structure is currently operated by the California Department of Parks and Recreation in partnership with the Robert Louis Stevenson Club—not that the spirits rumored to live there care one way or another.

The two-story adobe building first opened as the French Hotel during the period when California was a part of Mexico. A sign still proclaims the older name attributed to the building in the 1800s. The building was originally owned by Jose Rafael Gonzalez, the administrator for the Custom House when California was a part of Mexico. He sold the building in 1856 to Don Jose Abrego, who in turn sold it to the Girardin family. The family used the space to rent rooms to visitors, and thus was born the French Hotel. During that period, it became a popular destination for travelers, hosting artists, government officials and famous authors. This, of course, included Robert Louis Stevenson, after whom the building is now named. Stevenson stayed at the hotel for only a short period of time, however, although Stevenson House has a number of the Stevenson family's personal effects on display.

Stevenson is among the many authors associated with Monterey County, along with Steinbeck, Kerouac and a host of others. Born in Scotland in the year 1850, Stevenson was the only son of Thomas and Margaret Stevenson. The famed author had not yet written *Treasure Island*, nor *Strange Case of Dr Jekyll and Mr Hyde*, for which he is well known, when he visited Monterey.

The author stayed in the Old French Hotel in 1879 from August to December while courting the lovely Fanny Van de Grift Osbourne, who would later marry him and whose portrait can still be found in the

Treasure Island and *Strange Case of Dr Jekyll and Mr Hyde* author Robert Louis Stevenson. *Knox Series.*

building. The courtship was a difficult one for Stevenson due to both health and money issues, not to mention the fact that Fanny was married at the time. While in Monterey, he wrote the novella-sized story *The Old Pacific Capital*, which was published in 1892 in the book *Across the Plains*.

He also sold a few articles to the Monterey newspaper, *The Californian*. Within a year, Fanny would obtain a divorce from her husband and marry Stevenson.

It isn't the ghost of Stevenson, however, that keeps the supernatural alive in the historic building, but rather the ghost of a woman thought

A painting of Robert Louis Stevenson, who stayed for a brief time at the old French Hotel in 1879. *Author's collection.*

Tourists are invited to visit the Robert Louis Stevenson House, which is now open to the public for walk-in visits. *Author's collection.*

to have been killed by typhoid fever during the period when Stevenson lived there.

Typhoid fever, or *Salmonella typhi*, is rare in industrialized nations, but the nasty illness continues to this day and is responsible for more than 200,000 deaths annually. Antibiotics are used to treat the disease now but were not available to the public in the 1800s. This led to a higher number of deaths at that time.

The Stevenson House is thought to be haunted by the spirit of Manuela. Her husband, Juan, contracted typhoid fever in the summer of 1879 and succumbed to the illness. Manuela, left with the building and all the bills, suddenly had her hands full. Her grandchildren were also sick with typhoid, although they managed to survive thanks to her diligent care. She herself wasn't as lucky. The same year as her husband, Manuela also succumbed. She died in late December 1879. Years later, however, her presence can still be felt in the building, according to a number of eyewitness accounts.

Stories of the haunted building include a weird smell, typically ascribed to disinfectants like carbolic acid, which would likely be found in the large hotel when Stevenson lived there and would be present when the Girardin family fell ill. A female spirit has been reported in the building dressed in a black gown with a high lace collar, usually near the nursery area. One such account in 1970 reported that the woman had been seen by a guide, who found the woman standing near the nursery upstairs, dressed in black and looking down at the bed where the Girardin grandchildren once slept. On second glance, the guide reported that the woman in black had vanished from sight. Other sightings over the years repeated this "there one second, gone the next" assertion, although descriptions of the spirit vary, with some saying that the ghost wore a white shawl over her dark gown.

A current employee recounted that she once witnessed a rocking chair begin to move on its own in one of the upstairs rooms. To this day, she remembers the incident vividly and has become convinced that there is a spiritual presence in the building. The upstairs area, which once housed Park Service caretakers and their families, is now closed to the public. This includes the room with the rocking chair, as well as the room once inhabited by Stevenson.

Manuela Girardin, some think, is destined to repeat the last month of her life within the walls of the Stevenson House, which she spent primarily taking care of her two young grandchildren. Many of the spiritual occurrences have been reported during the month of December—in fact, the very month Manuela died.

A few accounts of spiritual occurrences are also ascribed to Stevenson himself, including one 1960s account of a woman and her sister who visited what was thought to be his rented room. Feeling the need to call for him, the woman spoke his name aloud and asked him to move things around if he was there. At that moment, a cold air descended around them, which the woman described as a chilly wind. The incident caused the woman to flee the room, although her sister remained a bit longer, obviously intrigued by what they believed to be a supernatural act.

Could it have been Robert Louis Stevenson himself answering a summons from beyond the grave?

THOSE WHO NEVER LEAVE STOKES ADOBE

A prominent two-story structure in downtown Monterey, Stokes Adobe is well known for being one of the city's most haunted buildings. The prominent location began as a single-room home built in 1833; the name would later be used for a popular local restaurant. In 1837, the home was purchased by an English sailor named James Stokes. Stokes was the town's druggist and doctor, although whether or not he was an actual doctor remained questionable, with most agreeing he only masqueraded as one, using medical supplies he stole from a boat he worked aboard. Despite this, he shot up in popularity as a local medicine man, and his practice prospered. His patients included then California governor Jose Figueroa. Stokes also became mayor of Monterey. A number of deaths were blamed on Stokes during his time as a local doctor, including that of Figueroa, who died a year after Stokes became his doctor.

Three years after taking ownership of Stokes Adobe, James married a widow with at least four, some say five, children. Josefa Soto de Cano went on to bear more children with James. According to some sources,

There is often a sense of something watching from the windows of Stokes Adobe, located in downtown Monterey. *Author's collection.*

they had up to five additional children together, although some claim they had only two. So many children meant the home had to grow, and so it did. For a decade, the old Mexican colonial bustled with activity due to the large family and the many events hosted at the site. The festivities wouldn't last, however. When Josefa died in the mid-1850s, James sold Stokes Adobe to a Frenchman named Honore Escolle, who owned the home until 1890. A kiln that Honore had converted from an oven could still be found on the property. It's thought to be the first kiln of its kind in California.

The Gragg family wins the honor of the family to own the building longest. They bought the building from Honore in 1890 and lived in it until 1940. Mortimer and Martha Harriet Gragg revived the parties once held there by the Stokes family, featuring any number of well-to-do guests, including author John Steinbeck. Martha, also known as "Hattie," was credited with reinstating the Stokes tradition, as the parties ceased once again when she died in 1948. Since that time, Stokes Adobe has operated primarily as a restaurant, including one of its most recent incarnations as Restaurant 1833. That restaurant closed silently in 2018, although some attributed the closure to the paranormal energies that seem to permeate the walls and grounds. The restaurant featured farm-to-table "American fare" in a posh atmosphere. Though closed permanently, ghost tours in Monterey still stop at the empty building, where chairs, aprons, glasses and even cash registers sat alone in a dark room after Restaurant 1833's closure.

Since at least 1950, and perhaps before, Stokes Adobe was the topic of a number of chilling tales, including sightings of the original owner himself, James Stokes. Rumors abound about James Stokes, including a belief that he hanged himself at the top of the stairs leading to the second-floor level. It's there where some reported seeing the ghostly image of a man dressed in attire from the 1800s. Others believe that the spirit is that of another man, although both remain mere speculation. People have also felt unseen hands tap them on the shoulder, been pushed and even shaken by what most believe was by the spirit of James Stokes. One report also tells the story of an employee closing the restaurant for the night. Having shut off the lights, locked the doors and walked to the parking lot to leave, the lights flicked back on in the building and the employee had to return once again to turn them off.

Hattie Gragg is also thought to haunt the old building. More than any other spirit, hers seems to cause the most mischief. She's been spotted, dressed in black, in both the kitchen and the upstairs area. It's been reported

The Monterey grave site of Maria Soto, wife of notorious con man James Stokes. *Author's collection.*

Many witnesses claim to have seen the spirit of a woman in vintage apparel on the Stokes Adobe property. *Drawing by Paul Van de Carr.*

that she has called out the names of current employees, who, upon looking around, see no one. Hattie has also been blamed for lifting a wine glass from a diner's hand and causing it to float a few feet on its own. Another account is of a candelabra that moved on its own across a grand piano, ultimately falling to the floor, although others attribute the incident to Stokes. Another report attributed to her is that of a woman seen running across the street toward the Stokes building. A driver, nearly hitting her, leaped from his vehicle to make sure the woman was okay, only to discover no one around. She seemingly vanished into thin air. Hattie's ghost is also known to play the piano once in a while. An apparition fitting Hattie's description has also been observed peeking out of the windows from behind the curtains, in the yard areas and on the balcony.

The home is something of a magnet for the paranormal, according to most accounts. Even Josefa's ghost is thought to haunt the old building. There have been reports of crashing noises, breaking glass, the voices of women talking and the sound of sobbing children from what was once Josefa's room. She's also been reported descending the stairs in a beautiful Spanish gown only to vanish into the air.

Perhaps due to the number of spiritual tales surrounding the old building, cold spots have been reported in various portions of the home, and some diners have even told wait staff that Stokes Adobe serves as a portal to the ghostly plane. Portals transporting spirits from one realm to another might very well explain the large number of paranormal incidents reported there.

Pictured is the unimposing front entrance of the Lara-Soto Adobe near downtown Monterey, found within walking distance of Old Fisherman's Wharf. *Author's collection.*

WHERE STEINBECK WROTE *THE PEARL* AND WHERE A BABY WAS BURIED

And the evils of the night were about them.

—*John Steinbeck,* The Pearl

The old Lara-Soto Adobe is unimposing and easy to miss as you drive down Pierce Street near downtown Monterey, but that nondescript demeanor hides a rich history, both supernatural and otherwise. This unassuming building once hid a terrible, dark secret. Built around the 1840s, the adobe was the property of Dona Feliciana Lara, one of the first female landowners in the region. The home was thought to be left vacant for a number of years before it became a home for criminals and vagrants, leading to its nickname as the "Bandit House." Rumors that the home was haunted started from the very beginning of the adobe's existence it seems. It was thought to sit vacant, not counting the criminal element, from 1860 to 1897, due to rumors of a supernatural presence there. In the 1920s, however, the home got a much-needed makeover.

Many believe that the adobe is not just a simple home, but rather the grave site of a three-year-old child who was buried just outside the front door. The little boy is thought to haunt the property to this very day. Some believe that a Monterey cypress tree was planted on the roadside of the land to mark the site. Today, the tree can still be found quite close to the property, within steps of where a porch had once been located. Unsubstantiated reports also claim that construction crews in the 1980s, while working on the property, unearthed what they believed to be the bones of a toddler, which seemed to confirm the story of the young boy. Rather than remove the remains, however, the property owner decided to rebury the bones back beneath the tree where he'd been unearthed.

The toddler's death, and the fact that he was buried not at a cemetery but in the yard outside the home, led many to believe that the home would be cursed forever. As it remained empty, used only by squatters, for many years, the curse seemed to be as good a reason as any for its state of ruin. In subsequent years, after the property was renovated, tales of haunted occurrences within its walls led one doctor, who used the home as offices, to usher out all staff and see no new patients after nightfall. He was simply too terrified to remain after dark. One story even tells of a security guard who heard what sounded like a party inside the home one evening, only to discover no one inside.

Besides its haunted tales, the home was also made famous thanks to author John Steinbeck, who purchased the adobe in 1944. It was here Steinbeck wrote the book *The Pearl*, historians said. But even Steinbeck, who was born nearby in Salinas, seemed to know of the property's ghostly presence and alleged curse. Before moving in with his wife and son, he enlisted the help of a priest to have the home exorcized of any demonic forces that might reside there. While living in Monterey, his book *Cannery Row* was published. Within a year, however, the family had moved out of the home and did not return. Historical accounts show that the family moved to Mexico to oversee production of *The Pearl* film. During that time, locals in Monterey were unhappy with the depiction of Monterey and its residents in *Cannery Row*. Steinbeck did not feel welcome returning to the area. What makes Steinbeck's short tenure at Lara-Soto Adobe so interesting is that the book *The Pearl*, which he wrote while living there, deals with the death of a boy, a story with striking similarities to the death that haunts the old adobe building.

Today, the residence is part of a number of properties owned by the Monterey Institute of International Studies. Local ghost tours stop at the Lara-Soto Adobe regularly, sharing the sad tale of the infant with visitors each year. Orbs, believed by many to be forms of spiritual energy, have been photographed often at this location and shared on travel review websites like Trip Advisor.

THE OLD MONTEREY JAIL AND THE HANGING TREE

Like the Lara-Soto Adobe, and within easy walking distance, the Old Monterey Jail sits with a sinister hanging tree located just outside. Today, the jail is a hub for tourists and Monterey historians eager to see a piece of the Central Coast's history. Remarkably, it looks much the same as it did when it was built in 1854 during the period of time when Monterey's courthouse was located in Colton Hall just next door.

Made of granite and iron, the jail used no wood in its construction, according to some historians, and allowed only the smallest of windows for prisoners to get a taste of fresh, free air. In 1935, the jail was upgraded with a heating and cooling system but remained largely untouched until it was closed in the late 1950s, just over a century after it was built. It has gone on to be an important part of Monterey's early history. Today,

The entrance to the Old Monterey Jail, which today is a draw for historians and tourists visiting the city's historic sites. *Author's collection.*

visitors can view the original cells, six in all, with bedding and other items found during that period. Some visitors, however, may get a little more than a history lesson. There have been reports of cold spots in the building, even a damp chill and foul odor, and some have seen a dark, shadowy shape within the building. The latter, according to some, may indicate the presence of the criminal Anastacio Garcia, who was imprisoned there for the murder of a lawman. A vigilante squad, it's said, sought revenge on Garcia and broke into the jail to mete out justice as they saw fit. He was killed outside the building, most believe, although some claim that he was killed on the balcony of Colton Hall (detailed a little later in this chapter).

Across the small street at the back of Colton Hall, within a stone's throw of the jail, one can still view the notorious hanging tree, where it's said many met their end thanks to the hangman's noose. The looming cypress tree can be found next to Vásquez Adobe. Orbs are photographed regularly at the tree, leading some to believe that they're the wandering spirits of those doomed souls, lost for an eternity at the grim site of their demise.

Like the hanging tree and the old jail, the neighboring Vásquez Adobe is also thought to house the spirits of the dead. While the Dutra

Considered one of the inspirations for the character of Zorro, criminal Tiburcio Vásquez was a well-known figure in old Monterey. *California State Library.*

Street property now belongs to the City of Monterey, the old building was once owned by Guadalupe Cantua de Vásquez, who purchased the home in the 1830s, although it underwent substantial renovations later. She's best known as the mother of Tiburcio Vásquez, one of the area's most renowned local bandits. Tiburcio, affectionately thought of as a sort of charming and sophisticated folk hero, is believed by many to be the original inspiration for the character of Zorro. (Others, however, believe that the famed bandit Joaquin Murrieta formed the inspiration for the character.) Vásquez was so sought after that the price on his head reached $6,000 dead or a whopping $8,000 if he were captured alive. Despite his allure, Tiburcio was eventually captured and hanged in San Jose for his various ill deeds, which included multiple murders, all before he hit the age of forty. Although he was kept and hanged in San Jose, he also spent time in the jail in Monterey, where some believe his spirit can still be found in his cell, just across the street from his mother's home. There is also rumor of a curse, made by Tiburcio just before he was hanged with a crucifix in his hand, against those who failed to protest his hanging. There were reports of rocks thrown by unseen forces against a San Jose resident shortly after the hanging, in fact, which a medium at the time attributed to the Vásquez curse.

But it isn't the spirit of Tiburcio that haunts his old home—it is that of his sister. The haunted adobe across the street is said to host her spirit on an almost nightly basis. Many have said that they've seen the figure of a young woman on the second-floor balcony, staring out into the night sky, which many attribute to Tiburcio's sister, who went on to own the building after their mother died. Flickering lights and the disturbing sounds of footsteps have also been reported in the Vásquez Adobe, as has a flushing upstairs toilet that seems to have a mind of its own. City employees working in the building have reported cold spots in the building and, more chilling, felt the presence of some invisible force moving past them. Often, footsteps can be heard upstairs when no one is around.

So haunted is this section of old Monterey that some claim there are ghosts on Dutra Street itself. Author Anita Yasuda shared a story of a woman waiting for her husband to retrieve his umbrella one afternoon and heard, while he was away, the creaking wheels of a stagecoach and the neighing of a horse. Strangely enough, no horses were in the area at the time. In fact, nothing was.

Colton Hall, located on Pacific Street and also near the old jail, is the site of California's statehood as the thirty-first state and where the state's

Pictured is the Vásquez Adobe in Monterey at dusk. Nearby is the notorious hanging tree, where a number of criminals met their end. *Author's collection.*

constitution was drafted in October 1849. While originally built with "chalk rock," or Carmel Stone, as a school and public offices, it also served as the courthouse; the site is now part of Monterey's historic past, serving as a museum, city offices and a research library. It's named for Reverend Walter Colton, a U.S. Navy chaplain, who was named as *alcalde*, or chief magistrate, of the Monterey area. In Spanish, *alcalde* means magistrate or mayor. Colton held that position from 1846 until California's statehood a few years later. He described the structure in *Three Years in California*, which he wrote in 1850:

> *Thursday, March 8, 1849. The town hall, on which I have been at work for more than a year, is at last finished. It is built of a white stone, quarried from a neighboring hill, and which easily takes the shape you desire. The lower apartments are for schools; the hall over them—seventy feet by thirty—is for public assemblies. The front is ornamented with a portico, which you enter from the hall. It is not an edifice that would attract any attention among public buildings in the United States; but in California it is without a rival. It has been erected out of the slender proceeds of town lots, the labor of the convicts, taxes on liquor shops, and fines on gamblers. The scheme was regarded with*

incredulity by many; but the building is finished, and the citizens have assembled in it, and christened it after my name, which will now go down to posterity with the odor of gamblers, convicts, and tipplers. I leave it as an humble evidence of what may be accomplished by rigidly adhering to one purpose, and shrinking from no personal efforts necessary to its achievement.

Besides the alleged hanging tree found in the back, many found guilty of crimes at the Colton Hall court were subsequently hanged from the second-floor balcony of Colton Hall. Many have reported the sounds of footsteps on the balcony, although no one has been there at the time. Guides and visitors have reported the eerie footsteps over the years, which they described as a slow shuffling, often likening the footsteps to the sort of shuffle someone would make while being walked to their painful death. Cold spots have also chilled visitors and employees who have walked through them, leading many to speculate about the spiritual presences found there. These cold spots are most prominent, people say, on the very balcony where these convicted criminals perished.

A Cursed Hotel

Before it became a part of the Naval Postgraduate School near the Seaside border of Monterey, one of the area's most haunted locations was a popular stopping point for travelers heading up and down the California coast. Named the Hotel Del Monte, its spacious accommodations sat on more than 120 acres of land, looked out on hundreds of lush trees and attracted the rich and famous alike. For sixty years, the hotel was a hot spot thanks to its spacious, ornate ballroom and breathtaking landscape. According to some reports, the hotel hosted more than fifteen thousand visitors per year, including presidents like Teddy Roosevelt and famous artists such as Salvador Dalí.

Established in 1880 near railroad land, the hotel was plagued by fires almost since its inception, leading many to believe the land to be cursed. A short seven years after it was opened, the hotel burned to the ground. But that didn't stop it from reopening, more ornate than ever, within a year following a quick construction period. This time, the hotel was built to hold seven hundred guests, up from its original four-hundred-guest

An 1883 postcard of Hotel Del Monte, which illustrated the grandeur of the now haunted local Monterey landmark. *San Francisco, H.S. Crocker & Company.*

capacity. Another fire burned through the Del Monte's Clubhouse in 1900 and then another in 1924. Rebuilt yet again, this time foregoing the Victorian design for a Mediterranean style, the hotel reopened in 1926. By 1950, the resort was struggling to make ends meet and was finally purchased by the Defense Institute for the navy's use. Oddly enough, the fires stopped when the hotel closed.

But the ghostly tales were just beginning. Over the years, there have been numerous stories of spectral encounters on the property. Staff with the Naval Postgraduate School has reported flickering lights, sensations of being tapped on the shoulder, unexplained movements and even an elevator that operates with a mind of its own. Others have reported ghostly sightings, particularly sighting of a "man in gray" and a woman dressed to the nines in elegant dinner attire. Another report indicated a ghostly visage near the hotel's 120-foot tower. Still others, however, believe that these stories were fabricated to entertain the wealthy hotel guests who flocked to the Bay. The fact that they are still shared and believed by many indicate how strongly they are felt in the community.

It's the man in gray who has been reported most over the years, although his identity has never been truly verified. Described as a middle-aged male in a gray suit, he has also been noted as having a gray beard or goatee and gray hair atop his head. Some believe this to be the spirit of David Jacks, one of the Monterey Peninsula's most notable landowners. Jacks is said to have once owned approximately 100,000 acres of land in Monterey County. Some of that land he sold, and it is on that property the hotel was soon constructed. Rumors indicate that Jacks became disenchanted with the development of the land he sold, however, and lamented that the Peninsula had become a playground primarily for the rich. Other legends claim that his land dealings didn't sit well with many of the native-born residents and that a curse was placed on him. Jacks is still remembered as a local icon, however, with Jacks Peak being named for his contribution to the Peninsula. Could it be his spirit that many have reported? While he fits a general description attributed to him by a waitress who reported a sighting of the gray man, some believe that the spirit is too playful to belong to what many described as a stern, serious man in David Jacks.

There have been numerous reports over the years of people feeling as though someone were tapping on their shoulder. When they turn around, no one is to be found, but the feeling of a finger on their shoulder was unmistakable. These reports have usually occurred in the area of the grand hallway and ballroom, according to accounts. The La Novia room has also been a hotbed of ghostly tales featuring the man in gray. Often, these shoulder taps have led to sightings of the ghost himself or flickering lights in some instances. While no one can be absolutely certain of the man in gray's identity, it's obvious to believers that he isn't going anywhere. Some, in fact, are quite comfortable with their "guest's" visits. For them, the ghost of the man is simply a part of life at the former grand hotel.

Yet he isn't the only ghost said to haunt the grounds. The mysterious figure of an ascending spirit has also been reported on more than one occasion. A firefighter battling the original fire in the 1800s, and who was never seen again, is often considered as a possibility when it comes to the identity of the spirit. Seen on more than one occasion, according to accounts shared by Reinstedt, a spirit was observed ascending into the air, as if walking on stairs to the rooms above. While there were no stairs there when the unusual occurrence was seen, stairs did exist in those locations originally. The first of these sightings was reported by a construction worker who was working alone when he saw the strange ascending spirit. When word got back to the firefighting community,

Monterey's Del Monte Beach is often full of people walking along the pristine shoreline, although some of them may not be mortal. *Author's collection.*

the crew agreed that the description of the ghost matched that of their missing comrade. A custodian also reported a similar occurrence that, according to Reinstedt's account, placed the appearance at around four o'clock in the morning, roughly the same time the fire broke out so many years before.

The nearby Del Monte Beach is said to be home to a number of wandering spirits as well. Often reported during periods of overcast weather, when gray fog rolls in to silently shroud the city, handfuls of lonely souls have been seen strolling along the sandy beach. These aren't men and woman out to walk the family dog, however, as these souls are dissipated, ephemeral beings whose faces are hard to make out. As they are dressed in gray pants and grimy shirts, some believe these spirits to be seafaring men who died at sea over the years. According to writer and ghost hunter Jeff Dwyer, who claimed to have seen a group of more than fifteen spirits himself, the four-mile stretch of beach, like the nearby hotel, is a hotbed for ghostly sightings. A woman dressed in Victorian-era swimming apparel, and visibly transparent, has been seen along the beach when the weather is gloomy and dark, according to Dwyer. Could these beings of the fog have drowned along this stretch of beach? Were they indeed sailors? Or were they former guests of the Hotel Del Monte? Only the tide, and perhaps the undertow, knows for certain.

MARINA'S LOST SOULS

While not as rich in paranormal history as Monterey, the beach town of Marina has its fair share of ghostly phenomena. Marina, which sits between Seaside and the city of Salinas, was once nine thousand acres of land owned by two men, David Jacks (who also owned the land where the Hotel Del Monte was located) and James Bardin. The Bardin family eventually sold portions of their land, leading to new landowners in the area. When the Southern Pacific Railroad laid tracks through town, life in the community began to change. Originally named Paddonville after San Francisco real estate salesman William Locke-Paddon, it was changed around 1918 to Marina. Paddon, it's said, didn't particularly enjoy having the area named for him and was himself partly responsible for the name change. Today, Marina is a bustling part of the Monterey Peninsula with a population of more than twenty thousand. Tourists visit the area, as do a number of Monterey County residents, for both the

The shadowy figure of what's thought to be a drowned surfer can sometimes be seen along the shore at Marina State Beach. *Author's collection.*

beaches and the shopping. Ghosts have also been rumored to exist within the community.

An apartment complex in Marina is one such eerie location. It is said to host the spirit of a young girl. Often seen standing alone in the hallway outside the apartments in a long black coat, this spirit has unnerved some residents to the point that they moved out. Besides her solitary appearances, the young girl is reported to scream in the middle of the night, rousing some residents from their deep slumber.

Near Marina State Beach, others have reported seeing a shadowy form along the shore. The shape walks with the gait of a person but looks more like a foggy outline than a human. Sightings of this ethereal form have been reported mostly in the early morning hours just before sunrise. Many speculate the ghost is that of a surfer who died there, while others believe it to be the spirit of a fisherman who frequented that section of the beach.

A spirit has also been reported on Paddon Place in Marina. Seen in a bonnet, the ghostly spirit has a passion for gardening. The spirit, according to one eyewitness who knew the area well, is believed to be that of Ione Olson, a beloved longtime Marina resident. Besides the bonnet, the spirit was dressed just as one would dress in the 1960s while tending to a garden, according to the eyewitness. Olson is a respected historical figure in Marina. An elementary school located on Beach Road is named for her.

Spirits of Old Fort Ord

It's not hard to get spooked at Fort Ord these days. Derelict buildings litter the Marina/Seaside border, some owned by California State University Monterey Bay (CSUMB), while much of the land became the Fort Ord National Monument. Many of the buildings were left to the elements and to time, not to mention bored teens with spray paint. Since Fort Ord's closure in 1994, many have explored the leftovers of the once historic base in Seaside. A rap video was even filmed among the abandoned barracks. In 2019, demolition crews worked to destroy many of these dilapidated structures.

At about twenty-eight thousand acres, the base primarily trained troops for active service. It was originally founded as Camp Gigling in 1917 and was designated as Camp Ord in the late 1930s following the addition of barracks, mess halls and administration buildings. In 1940, its name was officially changed to Fort Ord. The closure was announced in 1990, although the U.S. Army retained roughly 5 percent of the property.

President Barack Obama in 2012 set aside more than fourteen thousand acres of the property for the national monument. "The protection of the Fort Ord area will maintain its historical and cultural significance, attract tourists and recreationalists from near and far, and enhance its unique natural resources, for the enjoyment of all Americans," said Obama in his April 20, 2012 proclamation. Besides CSUMB and the national monument, the area is also home to a strip mall, a veterans facility and more.

In all, more than 1.5 million people went through Fort Ord's rigorous basic training program, including notable celebrities such as Jimi Hendrix and Clint Eastwood.

Tales of the supernatural have been whispered about the sprawling old property, including stories of barking dogs in the dead of night. These aren't simply loose canines wandering the trails and crumbling

Soldiers at Fort Ord run drills in this photograph from 1951. The property is now mostly owned by California State University–Monterey Bay (CSUMB). *California State University Monterey Bay.*

concrete sidewalks around Fort Ord, but rather spirit dogs whose guttural howls chill you to the bone. These dogs are believed to be the ghosts of the military service dogs thought to be buried somewhere near the barracks near Imjin Road. Many were buried there, according to Fort Ord historian Howard Gustafson. While there are no official sightings of ghost dogs, some have reported hearing their eternal cries in the middle of the night.

Soldiers living in the barracks from as far back as the 1940s are believed to still dwell there, many having committed suicide due to the stresses of basic training. Some believe that their spirits still haunt the now derelict buildings. Other reports have indicated the presence of military men wandering the forests and parks around the old military base to this day. Others claim that the dark shapes moving in the dark are merely homeless men and women, who can be seen living along the trails as well.

One of Fort Ord's well-known paranormal stories, however, takes place in a residential area once reserved for officers. The homes, many duplexes, are now used as residential properties for CSUMB staff, students and others. This particular home was rebuilt on a former base home. New construction or not, the haunting reported there doesn't seem bothered. It bothered the family who dwelled there, however, as they contacted the California Paranormal Research organization. The homeowners told tales of a number of chilling phenomena, including a shapeless shadow that was observed walking into the garage area, sounds of footsteps and, intriguingly, a male voice speaking to the family's child while she was alone in the upstairs bedroom.

According to their report, voices were recorded at the home, although little else was discovered. Multiple voices were recorded, both male and female, with one reported to say, "You have to come and help us." Another perhaps more playful voice said, "I'm Casper the Ghost."

Could these ghosts be former residents? With so many having once lived on the base, during Fort Ord's heyday, many think it's possible.

CSUMB grew from the ashes of Old Fort Ord, beginning in 1994 when former CSUMB executive Dean Hank Hendrickson signed the deed for the property on August 29. A few months later, CSUMB adopted a vision statement for the college that documented the school's core values, its philosophy in education and its scholarly aspirations. President Bill Clinton even paid a visit to the newborn campus in 1995 when classes began. While still surrounded by the relics of old Fort Ord, the school continued to blossom over the years.

Pictured are the ruins of what remains of Fort Ord today. Other areas are used for the CSUMB campus and shopping plazas. *Author's collection.*

While the remains are sprinkled about campus, new growth has also lined the landscape, as have the addition of new majors and other educational programs offered there, not to mention new college athletic teams. State-of-the-art classrooms and residence halls were also constructed, although that hasn't stopped the stories of hauntings. While some have been reported in the school, it's commonly thought that the phantoms hail from the days when soldiers, not students, were the norm on the property.

One former student, now an education professional who works in the Monterey area, shared her story of hauntings on the CSUMB campus when she was a liberal studies major. As far as she knows, these mysteries were never solved and likely still happen to the new generation of graduates toiling away on their school work.

In the spring of 2004, the former student said that she was a happy teen due to the fact she had her own room in the dormitories, a luxury not afforded to everyone. She was also employed as a resident advisor (RA) who served other CSUMB college students. As an RA, she got a stipend for food, room and board, not to mention a small paycheck. She often kept her dorm room door open so residents could pop in to ask questions if need be. One particular day, she was at work in her room when she heard a knock at the door. She didn't look up from her homework, however, and simply told the person to come in. She could hear the footsteps and even the sound of someone seating themselves on her bed. Thinking it was her boyfriend, she talked about her day and her homework assignments. After a few minutes, she realized there was no reply. At that point, she became nervous and said that the hairs on the back of her neck went up. She realized, despite the feeling and sounds indicating that she was most definitely not alone—that someone *was* with her—there was no one in the room. Being a Sunday, she knew that there were very few students on campus. After a few minutes, she heard the person get up and leave. Her door opened and closed. She remained at her desk, however, frozen with a cold fear. This lasted for only a few seconds, after which she leaped to her feet to see what she could see in the hallway. There was no one there. She ran down the stairs to the first floor in the hopes that she might see someone leaving the premises. She saw nothing there as well.

That same year, she found herself in a friend's dorm room, where she was sitting on a bed watching the *Buffy the Vampire Slayer* tv show. As she enjoyed the once-trendy show from the comfort of her friend's mattress, she saw a sweater on the back of a chair nearby. It was moving as if someone had brushed it walking by. She found the movement odd, and when she looked down saw what appeared to be military boots at the base of the chair, as if someone were sitting there. When she looked up again, she saw an image of a military uniform. Before she could see a face, however, the image disappeared. The sweater on the back of the chair, however, continued to move, as did the chair, which rocked back and forth. This was the second of three chilling tales recounted by just one former student.

In the fall of 2004, she experienced a third supernatural event on the former base turned campus. While still an RA for one of the dorms, part of her duty was to patrol the rooms and halls. She was considered on duty from five o'clock at night until the morning for some of her shifts. Her other duties included answering phones, monitoring the front desk, enforcing the rules and other duties. She was also tasked with making sure that the doors were secured at night. One night, she heard a thudding against one of the windows on the emergency exit door, located on the second floor, of what was known as Building 210 as she made her rounds. When she went to investigate the abnormal noise, she saw nothing there. Thinking it was merely students playing a trick, she pressed her forehead to look through the glass, thinking that she would see students hiding under the window, but saw no one there when she looked. She turned around and headed back down the hallway, only to hear the thudding against the door once again. The sound grew so loud that she feared the glass on the door would shatter, sending shards across the floor. Rather than investigate further, however, she turned and ran as any sane person would. Minutes later, she told another RA what had occurred. He also checked the door but found no sign of damage or anyone else for that matter. To this day, she believes that the sounds emanated from something not quite of this earth.

One Spirited Lighthouse

One of the West Coast's oldest active lighthouses is the small-statured Point Pinos Lighthouse. Located in Pacific Grove on Asilomar Avenue, it points its beacon to the sea at the western tip of Monterey Bay. Erected in 1855, the lighthouse isn't as tall as others along the California coastline, but it's just as memorable, particularly to the visitors who flock to the building each year. It was built, according to Dr. Lucy Neely McLane, of granite quarried from the property. The lighthouse was once lit continuously, serving as a guide for ships traveling along rocky coastal waters. Crews added a shutter in 1912, which allowed the light to be on for ten seconds and off for twenty seconds. Called a signature, the lighthouse is now known for being on three seconds out of every four seconds. It's also fully automated these days.

Attached to the Point Pinos Lighthouse is a Cape Cod–style bungalow that once housed the building's first keeper, England native Charles Layton, who lived there with his wife and four children. Layton would die in his first year, however, due to his side work as part of the local constabulary and sheriff's posse. Layton was killed while working to apprehend the aforementioned Anastacio Garcia. With Layton's untimely

Point Pinos Lighthouse as it appeared in 1871. The lighthouse looks much the same today, although it's now surrounded by more structures. *Photo by historical photographer Edward James Muggeridge.*

death at Garcia's hands, his family was left with very little money. His wife, Charlotte, however, soon became the new keeper of the lighthouse, despite the fact that it was largely unheard of for a woman to hold such a title at the time. Charlotte would remain keeper until 1860, when she remarried. Other lighthouse keepers over the years include Captain Allen Luce and longtime keeper Emily Fish.

In 1879, author Robert Louis Stevenson visited the lighthouse during his sojourn at Monterey at the French Hotel, another haunted site along the Central Coast. Stevenson's own grandfather invented the system of flashing lights used in lighthouses. The author himself apprenticed as a lighthouse engineer in his younger years and met with Luce at the time.

In 1906, the year of the great San Francisco Earthquake, the little lighthouse in Pacific Grove suffered heavy damage, leading to the complete rebuild of the tower seen there today. This, and the Second

World War, were some of the only times the lighthouse went dark. In the war, the lighthouse was shut off intentionally to conceal its location on the chance that enemy ships roamed the seas nearby. This didn't deter some, however, as it is said a Japanese submarine shot at the lighthouse's lens during the war.

While Layton was killed in a brutal attack, it is not his ghost that haunts the popular lighthouse, but that of Emily Fish. A native of

The lighthouse at Point Pinos isn't as tall as others on the coast. After the 1906 earthquake in San Francisco damaged the structure, the diminutive tower had to be completely rebuilt. *Author's collection.*

Michigan, Fish was born in 1843 and moved west after her marriage to Dr. Melancton W. Fish. She became the lighthouse keeper after her son-in-law told her of the vacancy. It was a role to which she would become attached. In fact, she can still be seen there to this day. Fish was known as a strict light keeper and is remembered for firing thirty incompetent male workers in the twenty-one years she worked as light keeper. She's also remembered as something of a socialite who held piano recitals and tea parties. Reports have indicated her ghostly presence in the lighthouse, dressed in a Victorian gown, but with features blurred to the point of barely being visible. Items left on tables also have a habit of being moved randomly, as if Fish continues to clean up after those visiting or working in the lighthouse.

Eerie noises have also been reported on the second floor of the lighthouse, as well as unidentifiable smells that some attribute to the spirit of Charlotte Layton, according to ghost hunter Jeff Dwyer. The sound of a "swooshing" dress has also been reported, as if an invisible woman in a gown were roaming the rooms. Could it be Charlotte? Or is Emily still going about her light keeping duties?

Doc Ricketts and the Lab

Ed "Doc" Ricketts was a marine biologist and good friend to local author John Steinbeck, who was born and raised in Monterey County. Edward Flanders Robb Ricketts for years made his home on what is now known as Cannery Row. His lab, where he collected marine specimens taken from tide pools in the area, can still be found amid the throng of tourists and vehicles next to the Monterey Bay Aquarium. Although featured in Steinbeck's writing as a character in the novels *Cannery Row*, *The Log from the Sea of Cortez*, *Sweet Thursday* and others, Ricketts was himself an author and avid reader. His books *Between Pacific Tides* and *Breaking Through: Essays, Journals, and Travelogues of Edward F. Ricketts* are still widely read to this day, particularly among marine life scholars.

Ricketts was born in Chicago in 1897. He made his way to the California coast and opened Pacific Biological Laboratories in 1923 with the help of his roommate, A.E. Galigher. He would meet Steinbeck in the year 1930, with the two becoming fast friends. Ricketts provided Steinbeck with the inspiration for the "Doc" character in *Cannery Row*, although many historians do not believe Ricketts himself should have Doc as a part of his name, since "Doc" was merely the character in Steinbeck's book. Ricketts is also credited with predicting the sardine "crash" that eventually befell Monterey County around 1950 due to possible environmental factors and overfishing in the Bay. The sardines wouldn't return to the Bay in large number until the mid-1990s.

Back in the 1930s, the decade in which he cemented his bond with Steinbeck and other local visionaries, including writer Henry Miller, Ricketts could often be found in his lab at 800 Cannery Row, as it's addressed today, among the many marine specimens he collected. Besides a marine biologist and owner of the laboratory and specimen supply company, he was also fondly remembered as both a philosopher and early environmentalist. Even after the original lab burned to the ground and became nothing more than a smoldering ruin, Ricketts remained a fixture on the Row. With a little financial help from his successful author friend and Salinas icon, he soon built a new lab and continued his scientific work at the edge of the sea. It's that structure that still stands to this day.

Cannery Row then was not the tourist mecca that it is today of course. At the time, Cannery Row featured more warehouses and canneries than tourists and traffic and smelled more of dried fish guts than fine dining and chocolate confections. It was a working sector back then, striving to prepare and can product for delivery by rail to a hungry population. At the time, the railroad cut a path along the shoreline and stretched to Lover's Point in Pacific Grove for years before service was discontinued in 1971.

He was still a part of Cannery Row in 1948 when he set out for dinner in his old Buick. It was May 8, and Ricketts was reportedly not paying attention and failed to see the Del Monte Express as the train made its way down the rail line. His car was struck where the tracks crossed Wave Street. It took first responders an hour to get him out of the mangled vehicle due to the severity of the crash. The impact didn't immediately kill him, however. Ricketts hung on for approximately seventy-two hours before finally passing away, ending the reign of one of Cannery Row's most iconic characters. He died only days from his fifty-first birthday.

After his death, the laboratory became the property of Yock Yee, who owned the Wing Chong Company, called Lee Chong's grocery store in Cannery Row, which operated right across the street next to the infamous Cannery Row brothel also featured in Steinbeck's unforgettable book. Yee

Pictured is famed local marine biologist Ed Ricketts as he collects specimens along the craggy shore, where he could be found most days in the 1930s and '40s. *Photo by George Robinson, courtesy National Steinbeck Center.*

owned the building for a handful of years but rented it out to tenants, which included Monterey High School literature teacher Harlan Watkins, who would go on to buy the building in 1956. While he lived in the lab for a short period, Watkins also held gatherings there for his group named for Ricketts, the Pacific Biological Laboratories Club (PBL Club for short). The club

The bust of Ed Ricketts along the recreation trail on Cannery Row can often be seen holding flowers. *Author's collection.*

bought the building in 1958, the same year the street outside was renamed from Ocean View Avenue to Cannery Row.

Tales of Ed Ricketts continued after his untimely demise, only with eerier undertones, and not the sort that had much to do with marine biology. Even now, visitors to the site have reported a distinct chill in the air at the spot where Ricketts was struck. Today, a bronze memorial bust of Ricketts (holding a starfish in his hand) can be found on the walking trail at the site, along with a railroad crossing sign, although the tracks

A local author once claimed to have observed a dark, shadowy figure emerge from the old Cannery Row laboratory that once belonged to Ed "Doc" Ricketts. *Drawing by Paul Van de Carr.*

have long since been removed. The Ricketts statue is a popular landmark on the Row, and visitors often place flowers in the statue's hand. It's at this spot where many have reported "cold spots"—areas where the temperature is considerably cooler than the air around it. While the reason for cold spots remains up for debate, many believe the energy needed to manifest a spiritual presence would pull from the heat nearby, thus dropping the temperature. Energy might indeed be needed if tales of mystery noises can be believed. Visitors to the site have reported the sounds of a train (when none is around) and wrenching metal. A female's voice and sobbing have also been reported at the scene of the crash. Some believe that these sounds are spiritual "memories" from the day Ricketts was struck, made by the large group of onlookers that showed up to mourn for the popular scientist.

Farther down the street, at the site of the wooden laboratory itself, eyewitnesses have reported seeing strange moving lights over the rickety front steps leading into the building. Jeff Dwyer, author of the book *Ghost Hunter's Guide to Monterey and California's Central Coast*, reported more than that, however. He reportedly observed a shadowy figure emerge from the building late one rainy afternoon on Cannery Row. The dark shape, with no discernible features, strolled down the stairs of the building before vanishing down the street. Accounts of shadowy beings have been reported in other parts of Cannery Row as well. Thought to be long-dead fisherman or cannery workers, these dark shapes have been seen walking up the hill away from the shoreline, as if heading home after a long day of work.

CHILLING STORIES OF PACIFIC GROVE, PEBBLE BEACH AND CARMEL

Many of Monterey County's ghostly encounters pertain to the area's rich historical context. Most of the city of Monterey is itself a site of great historical relevance, to the state of California as well as to Spain and Mexico. It's no surprise that these areas have a deep well of ghost stories as nuanced and spectacular as the Peninsula itself.

Pacific Grove was originally founded as a Methodist Church retreat in 1875. With Point Pinos Lighthouse already established, work began on Lighthouse Avenue, connecting the bustling port of Monterey with this wooded area ideal for camping. With the arrival of the Southern Pacific

Railroad, the community of religious campers began to blossom. The city was incorporated in 1889. Today, the community of more than fifteen thousand residents is home to the annual migration of monarch butterflies and known by the moniker of "America's Last Hometown." Ed Ricketts lived in Pacific Grove for a time, as did John Steinbeck and other notable American icons. Robert Louis Stevenson, during his extended visit to the Peninsula, remarked on Pacific Grove in his book *The Old Capitol*, "I have never been in any place so dreamlike. Indeed, it was not so much like a deserted town as like a scene upon the stage by daylight, and with no one on the boards."

Its dreamlike qualities may explain the number of tales that have sprung up over the years—tales of those long dead but that refuse to leave their earthly connection to the land. Pacific Grove's tranquil environment, hometown vibes and seasonal monarch butterfly population may be what prevent so many residents from living anywhere else. Why move when you're already living in paradise? This could be the reason why so many of its Victorian-era homes are said to be haunted by former residents of the city. For them, too, there's no place like Pacific Grove. Victorian homes aren't defined by architecture so much as by the era in which the homes were built, namely the Victorian era, in which Queen Victoria held court over Britain, from about 1837 to 1901. Homes built in Pacific Grove during this time fall under this classification, although there are many variations to the Victorian "style," including Queen Anne, Stick, Shingle and the fancy-named Richardsonian Romanesque. Spotting a Victorian home is easy, although many have been refurbished over the years. Simply look for a steep roof, many angles to the home and a full asymmetrical porch typically found at the front or side of the home. Their often Gothic appearance makes the belief in local hauntings that much easier to swallow.

One Victorian home, near downtown P.G., is home to a mysterious, strange face that peers from the walls. The man doesn't stare at anything in particular, it's said, but merely stares at something only he can see. Other haunted homes have pictures removed from the walls at night and placed, facedown, on the floor, according to local ghost hunter Reinstedt. Tales have also been told of a home near the shore that hosts the spirit of a long-dead sea captain. His ghost can sometimes be seen pacing the porch and looking longingly toward Monterey Bay. One resident on Lighthouse Avenue recounted a tale that included the sound of someone pacing on the floor above him. Voices could also be heard. To top off an already terrifying evening, his bed began to tremble while he lay in it, attempting to ignore the noises and go to sleep. Suddenly, his comforter was ripped from the bed, forcing the man to his feet. The evening and subsequent nights, he said, brought similar unexplained incidents. In another Pacific Grove home, residents moved after a particular room drove the family to seek new accommodations. There, reports of screaming, scratching at the walls and moans would often startle the family who lived there. They even recorded the sounds on a cassette player at the time and could hear the screams when they played it back. A Victorian home on Alder Street is also said to be haunted by shy ghosts that never show themselves but can often be heard walking around in the home when the resident is asleep in bed. The front door has opened and closed as well, as if these ghosts are often out running errands.

A local resort hotel has also had its share of odd occurrences in the dead of night. Visitors to the small community between Pebble Beach and Monterey have reported the sounds of running water all night and, more disturbing, related troubling nightmares with almost identical stories upon waking. Some of these stories can be found on travel review sites, offering the chilling question to readers, "Room 107—Haunted?"

Deer enjoy the wet grass at the cemetery in Pacific Grove, California, the site of a number of ghostly sightings. *Author's collection.*

The old cemetery has also been the topic of ghostly conversations over the years. This includes dark sightings in the fog, of which there are numerous accounts of ethereal forms appearing and disappearing in the suffocating mist. Another account is that of a little boy that appears when his grave is touched, only to vanish when called away by the spirit of his long-dead mother.

Pebble Beach, simply called "Pebble" by locals, is well known for its golf, luxurious homes, scenic 17-Mile Drive and private entrances. Located between Pacific Grove and Carmel-by-the-Sea, Pebble Beach started as part of a land deal between Samuel Finley Brown Morse and the Pacific Improvement Company. Morse managed the company at the age of twenty-nine and formed the Del Monte Properties Company, which included eighteen thousand acres of land. Today, with the name changed to the Pebble Beach Company, the community remains one of the Peninsula's most treasured gems.

One of the community's darker attractions, and a well-known ghost in the Monterey Peninsula, is the Lady in Lace, often seen on the Pebble Beach stretch of 17-Mile Drive after the sun has set and darkness has settled over the roadway. Reports have placed the wandering female spirit near the popular Ghost Tree landmark, at Pescadero Point, where she's often been caught in the headlights of terrified motorists driving past, appearing in the centerline of the road or at the edge of the rocks overlooking the turbulent sea. The woman disappears from sight after each appearance. Not to be confused with the Lone Cypress, the Ghost Tree is a popular spot for surfers and visitors alike. Whether the Lady in Lace notices these things is open for debate. Some have reported that the lace in question is a wedding gown and that this woman was a jilted lover, destined forever to relive the worst day of her life. Others believe she's the ghost of Dona Maria del Carmen Barreto, who owned much of the land where Pebble Beach is now located after inheriting the land from her husband. She later sold the land for a paltry sum, roughly twelve cents per acre, and moved to Monterey. The dress, which many say is merely a formal gown popular in the 1920s, is not a wedding dress at all but does indicate the period and wealth of the woman at the time of her death. They say that Dona Maria regretted her sale after she moved to Monterey and thus continues to visit what was once her property to this day.

Carmel-by-the-Sea, simply called "Carmel" by residents, borders on Pebble Beach, and is home to numerous phantasmagorical accounts, including the Carmel Mission and Tor House, which have their own chapters devoted to them. But there are other stories about this charming hamlet made internationally famous when actor Clint Eastwood was elected mayor there in the late 1980s.

Before Eastwood was a household name, men like Spanish explorer Sebastián Vizcaíno sailed the seas. Vizcaíno is thought to have been one of the first Europeans to set foot on the Peninsula after arriving in Monterey Bay in 1603. He traveled to the area where Carmel is today and there found a beach and river, which historians claim he called Carmelo to honor the three Carmelite friars who traveled with him on his voyage. Just under two hundred years later, Junípero Serra would settle there as a second location for his system of missions dotting the California coast. In the 1900s, cypress trees were added to the landscape in an effort to add to the area's quaint charm. Soon the area became a hotbed for artists seeking to capture the beauty of the land. Following the devastation of the 1906 earthquake in San Francisco, many of the artistic souls, writers, poets and painters who once simply visited the area moved there for good as a way to escape the quake-damaged Bay Area. Besides notables like Robinson Jeffers, featured in the chapter on the Tor House, other notable authors to move to the area include Jack London and George Sterling. The city incorporated in 1916. Today, Carmel is a hotbed of activity, featuring five-star restaurants, daily celebrity sightings and high-end shopping, while retaining its quaint, cottage-like atmosphere. Those who stay at the many inns and hotels in Carmel, hoping to soak in the charm of the city, may find themselves getting more than they bargained for.

One particular inn in Carmel has had its fair share of haunted tales. According to some of the reports, the encounters were so terrifying that the inhabitants fled the room in the middle of the night. The first occurred after dark when a couple ordered room service. They began to hear odd noises in the room that were not coming from them. This included footsteps and the sound of people laughing. As the evening wore on, the couple heard the fridge open and close in the room, followed by what sounded like a bottle rolling down stairs. Having had enough, the two packed their bags and checked out. Others have reported similar accounts, including the presence of a spirit that shook the bed and even of a paralysis that made the guest unable to move. A presence was also reportedly felt on the bed, as if an invisible weight had been placed there.

More than one inn in the beautiful beach community has had reports of uninvited company from beyond. In one instance, at another inn on Ocean Avenue, a man and a woman were watching television one evening in their

A portrait of Alida Ghirardelli taken from the May 30, 1909 edition of the *San Francisco Call* newspaper.

room, his head in her lap. The man reported the feeling of fingers running through his hair, while the woman said she observed a dark, shadowy form in her peripheral vision at the same time. The shape, and the sensation, vanished immediately when the man asked the woman if she had been touching his hair. She said she hadn't but told him about the dark shape she observed floating just above him.

One hotel, Carmel's fabulous La Playa, is thought to be haunted by Alida Ghirardelli. The hotel was built in 1905 as a home for artist Chris Jorgensen and his wife, chocolate heiress Angela Ghirardelli. Her niece, Alida, would often head to the beach from the home and spend the afternoon frolicking in the pristine surf. One day, however, Alida never returned. It was soon discovered that she'd drowned in the sea after being pulled under by a surprise undertow, which can often occur along the Monterey shore. The tragedy led Angela and Chris to pack up and move out of Carmel and back to the big city up north. Angela would pass away in 1936, one year after her husband died, and many said she never fully recovered from the death of Alida.

Today, many believe that the ghosts of both Alida and Angela frequent the hotel's lush property. Both have been seen on the property dressed in the attire of the era, although Alida is typically spotted in a bathing outfit with wet hair. The two have been spotted over the years walking in the beautiful garden or standing on the terrace. What compels them to stay is anyone's guess, although it could simply be that they enjoy spending their eternity together in their former home.

A short drive from Carmel, one finds the hamlet of Carmel Valley. This rural community sits between Salinas and Carmel alongside the Carmel River and is accessed primarily from the winding Carmel Valley Road. Deep in the Valley, along the remote San Carlos Road, one may hear the tale of the dead rancher, a man many have reported seeing in the middle of the night. Wearing an old sweater that looks gray in the darkness, crusty jeans and cowboy boots, the rancher is often reported holding a lantern as he ambles around an old shed. Many who've seen him believe he's trying to feed horses that were once stabled there in a barn, but like him, those horses have long since died.

SERRA'S MISSION

When Father Serra moved Mission San Carlos Borromeo to Carmel from its former location facing Monterey Bay in 1771, he was quite familiar with the Native American communities that inhabited the area. The area's original inhabitants weren't too happy with their new neighbors in those early days. The Spanish soldiers treated the local population harshly, according to historians, which angered Serra and led to his decision to move the mission into what is now Carmel-by-the-Sea, called "Carmel" for short, to put a little distance between the mission and the soldiers.

While many call the impressive mission compound simply the Carmel Mission, its full name is in honor of the Italian patron saint of Spain's King Charles III, Carlos Borromeo. The mission in Carmel was the second to be built in California. Twenty-one missions, used by the Spanish to convert native populations to Christianity and other uses, were built in all. At the time, the mission system was a way for the Spanish to control new territories.

The Carmel Mission was considered the head mission for California at that time, as Serra, being president, made his headquarters there. Serra also founded the first of California's missions in San Diego in 1769. With a rich history like the mission's, ghostly appearances and spiritual phenomena have become as regular as Sunday mass.

One particular eerie tale, reported often by ghost hunters and historians like Randall A. Reinstedt, concerns a man seen long ago, on multiple occasions, riding near the grounds of the mission. This man rode a white horse and was unidentifiable to those who long ago witnessed the horseback rider. They could only say that the rider appeared to be in a hurry and was always riding south toward the Santa Lucia Mountains astride his glowing white stallion. Some believe that this ghostly apparition belonged to a Spaniard scout thought to be connected with the Portolá expedition in search of Monterey Bay. Others have claimed this rider to be headless, similar to the legend of the headless horseman but with a Spanish twist. Some believe the spirit is that of Joaquin Murrieta, often called the Robin Hood of El Dorado. Murrieta was a famous cowboy, rogue and gold miner from around the 1850s. While there are a number of stories surrounding him, many are considered myths. Remember he is also the man many consider to be the real-world inspiration for the character of Zorro. Could it be he is the mysterious horseman?

This oil painting offers a striking portrait of Father Junípero Serra. Serra was born on November 24, 1713. *Wikimedia Commons.*

Among the stories of spectral visitors to the mission are tales of a Native American boy seen frequently on the hallowed grounds. Others claim to have seen a nameless priest over the years wandering the halls from the mission's Convento Museum to the Jo Mora Chapel Gallery, as well as a spirit dog that vanishes at will. The graveyard, which visitors and church officials have often noted for its spiritual ambiance, is the final resting place for what's believed to be the bodies of thousands of Mexicans, Americans and natives, as well as church officials, the latter of whom are marked with headstones. Many have reported feeling "cold spots" and even touched by cold, invisible hands while touring the cemetery area.

Perhaps best known, however, is the ghost of Saint Junípero Serra himself. Accounts of his solemn apparition on the mission grounds are numerous. Serra died in Carmel-by-the-Sea on August 28, 1784. Some say that he returns to say mass every year during the Feast of San Carlos. The event honors Saint Charles Borromeo, for whom the mission is named, with a feast in his name. Serra himself founded nine missions in California; the Carmel Mission was his favorite. He lived there in a small room. When he died at the mission in the year 1784, he was given a prominent burial on the grounds. Sightings of fog-like beings have been reported ever since Serra died, particularly during the Feast, and even after the old adobe church where Serra was buried was rebuilt using stones quarried from the Santa Lucia Mountains.

The legend of Serra's ghostly visitations is so popular, in fact, that it was even written about in a poem by Richard Coward called "The Midnight Mass":

Today, the Carmel Mission remains a religious monument and tourist attraction for travelers passing through the Monterey Peninsula. *Author's collection.*

Tales are told and songs are sung
Of Junipero the Padre
In the sweet Castilian tongue:
Telling how each year he rises
From his grave the mass to say,
In the midnight, 'mid the ruins,
On the eve of Carlos' day.
THE MIDNIGHT MASS.

Today, the mission hosts regular church services, including weddings, and throngs of visitors come to see its museum, grounds and gift shop every day.

WHO'S HAUNTING TOR HOUSE?

Alone with open eyes in the clear air growing old,
Watching with interest and only a little nausea
—excerpt from the poem "The Old Stone-Mason" by Robinson Jeffers

Poet Robinson Jeffers liked the idea of living within stone walls and jumped at the chance to create his own fortress of impenetrable solitude. It was here where he wrote most of his poetic works. Jeffers built the home for his wife and twin sons and continued to make improvements and additions to the site, located in Carmel near Scenic Road and not far from the Carmel Mission, for many years. Jeffers also built the four-story Hawk Tower on the property, which offers a breathtaking view of Central Coast landscape and the Pacific Ocean beyond. Originally intended to be a cottage for his family, the home contained two attic bedrooms, one bathroom, a cramped living room and kitchen and a guest room found on the main floor. Jeffers later added another wing, as well as a dining room, to the home. He built Hawk Tower himself, which took him a little over four years to complete, as a retreat for him and his wife.

Born in Pennsylvania in 1887, Jeffers spent much of his childhood traveling abroad, although he eventually returned to America to enroll in college at the University of Pennsylvania. He graduated from higher education courses at eighteen. Later, he met fellow graduate student and musician Una Call Kuster. The two married in 1913. By the mid-1920s,

Pictured is the poet Robinson Jeffers. *Library of Congress, Prints & Photographs Division, Carl Van Vechten Collection, reproduction number LC-USZ62-54231.*

Jeffers had become a well-known poet with his collection *Tamar and Other Poems*. Having traveled to the Central Coast, he and his wife fell in love with the area's abundant natural beauty.

Jeffers bought the land where Tor House stands today with money from an inheritance. They began building their new home in 1919. He finished Hawk Tower, complete with a dungeon-like basement, in 1924. Like the nearby Carmel Mission, Jeffers originally planned to use stone quarried from the nearby Santa Lucia Mountains. Due to the rocky terrain found in the vicinity of Carmel Point, which reminded Jeffers and his wife, Una, of the tors found in Dartmoor, England, they opted to use the rocks around them. Tor House was born. Jeffers would go on to plant thousands of trees on the property, including Eucalyptus, pine and cypress trees. Many of those trees can still be found on the property.

Jeffers would spend his mornings writing in Tor House's upstairs loft. During these literary endeavors, he'd sit on an antique chair made from wood that once made up the original adobe structure of the Carmel Mission. Jeffers himself said he could feel the spiritual residue left by the mission in the years when it had become all but deserted. These spirits, he believed, came from the native peoples who inhabited the land in Carmel. In fact, it's said that Jeffers uncovered ancient fire pits on his property when he started construction of Tor House.

Today, Tor House offers tours and special events that celebrate Jeffers and his family. The nonprofit Robinson Jeffers Tor House Foundation operates the property as part of the National Trust for Historic Preservation. Its mission is to "preserve Tor House, Hawk Tower and their collections, to promote the literary and philosophical legacy of Robinson Jeffers for the enrichment and enlightenment of the public, and to serve the community as a cultural resource."

But historians and fans of the Jeffers family aren't the only inhabitants on the property. Many believe that a spirit can be found within the stone walls of Tor House. While some believe that Jeffers himself haunted the home and Hawk Tower, it's now commonly thought that his wife, Una, is the restless spirit. The haunting is so well known that Tor House was named one of the top thirteen haunted locations along the California coast on the California Beaches website. Its spirit-filled presence has also been featured on the show *Ghost Adventures*.

The show's producers, not to mention a few Jeffers enthusiasts, believed at the time that Jeffers would make his presence known approximately fifty years after he died. Jeffers hinted at just such an appearance in his

Pictured is Hawk Tower, built by the poet Robinson Jeffers as a retreat for him and his wife, Una Call Kuster. *Photo by Celeste Davison.*

poem "Ghost," in which he wrote he would haunt the property. While Jeffers himself made no appearance, there have been reports over the years of a haunted presence. An administrative assistant reported one ghostly encounter to the *Carmel Pine Cone*, in which she told the newspaper that a particular book repeatedly fell from a bookshelf. That book was about Una Jeffers. When the assistant finally read the book, it stopped falling from the shelf.

PART II
BEYOND THE BAY

SALINAS NORTHRIDGE AND OTHER HAUNTED HOT SPOTS

The land in what is now known as the Salinas Valley was once solely inhabited by Native American tribes, which included the Costanoan, Ohlone, Salinan and Esselen tribes. Salinas is sitting in what was then primarily Ohlone, Costanoan land. The tribe were hunters and gatherers but also relied on acorn crops that grew in the fertile land in the Valley. Four of the state missions began to appear on their lands in the 1700s, beginning with the first mission in Monterey in 1770. Three others soon followed: the Mission San Antonio de Padua in 1771, Mission Soledad in 1791 and the Mission San Juan Bautista in 1797.

In 1822, when Mexico gained independence from Spain, settlers began to arrive in the area in droves. They came to the land by any means of travel available to them. Salinas became the center of Monterey County by 1872 thanks to the new blood flooding into the region. Two years later, the city incorporated. By this time, work had already begun on expanding the Valley as a hub for the nation's agricultural needs, despite a devastating drought that dried up the land in the community from 1897 to 1898. The residents, determined to make a go of life on the coast, soon rebounded and sought once again to become America's agricultural center. That desire was cemented when, during this same period, the Southern Pacific Railroad laid tracks through the community. By the end of World War I, the produce grown in the Salinas Valley had become known as "green gold," leading to the city's nickname as the "Salad Bowl of the World."

In 1890, Salinas boasted a population of more than 2,300 residents, making it one of the largest communities in the area. Despite the Great Depression that hit the industrialized world from 1929 to 1939 and displaced families all over the country, Salinas continued to thrive. That population continued to grow, particularly after the construction of Highway 101 through the city in 1915. By 1920, the population had doubled to more than 4,300. The city attracted families from all over the world, including Japanese families, Filipino families and more. Today, census numbers place the population of Salinas at over 157,000 in 2016. Currently, the city's more than $2 billion economy produces approximately 80 percent of the country's lettuce and artichokes, not to mention other crops produced in the Valley.

It's the Valley's prime climate for agriculture that helped usher in an era of prosperity on the Central Coast, one that attracted families to move there from all across the country. New construction sprang up in the community, incorporating modern Art Deco designs to illustrate the wealth of the city in the early 1900s. The Salinas Californian Building is one such example of this form of architecture—and one of the area's haunted locales as well.

The city's popular shopping center, Northridge Mall, was created in answer to the rapidly increasing population. It has also been the site of a ghostly encounter that might very well date back to a time when only Native Americans occupied the surrounding land. Mall staff and security personnel have on numerous occasions reported a strange female presence in the large complex, which opened in 1974 and remains open today. The mall offers more than one hundred shops and is spread out over nearly 100,000 square feet. Described as a Native American woman, the ghostly figure has often been observed wandering the area during off hours. Some believe her to be the lost spirit of one of the city's original inhabitants, from a time when the area was primarily Ohlone land. What unfortunate incident befell her, leaving her trapped on the property for eternity, only she can answer.

There are many haunted locations in the community, particularly in the downtown historic district, some of which will be explored in greater detail

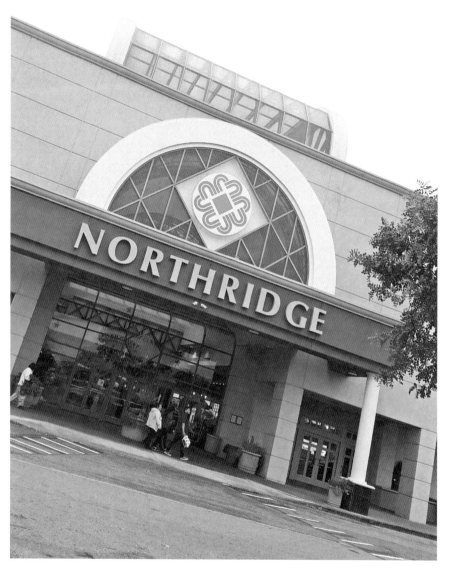

The popular Northridge Mall in Salinas is said to be home to the spirit of a Native American woman. *Author's collection.*

later. One such haunting concerns a home located on Central Street near the house formerly occupied by the Steinbeck family, where author John Steinbeck was born. A witness there reported multiple sightings of a woman dressed in black Victorian apparel. She was often observed staring through a window toward the Steinbeck home. Other shadowy figures have also been observed on the property, which is now a multiple-residence structure, and disembodied voices are often heard in the attic, despite the fact that no one was up there at the time. On one occasion, hands were visible coming through a window, according to the eyewitness account, although the window was located on the second floor of the building with no access except for a ladder, which was not there.

An apartment on Natividad Road is also home to a number of spooky encounters that have left the locals feeling a bit shaken when they tuck into bed at night. Located near an old cemetery, some residents have reported odd phenomena, including figurines on shelves that are often turned around facing the wall and photos of family members falling from the walls regularly to shatter and crash on the floor. Some photos, according to accounts, have even been "flung" from the walls, according to testimonies shared online. Not far from there, another haunted tale befell residents at a separate apartment complex fashioned from an old home on West Alisal Street. One woman shared her account on an online message board—it could only be described as a year of terror. From nearly the moment she moved into the apartment, remarkable incidents began to occur. She'd hear footsteps outside her door in the apartment's lobby, and when she checked through the peephole of her apartment, thinking that she'd see one of her neighbors, no one would be there. On one occasion, she heard the distinct sound of those same footsteps, only they were coming from her bedroom. A man's "grumbling" could be heard on other occasions when she believed she was the only one in the apartment at the time. Physical manifestations began to materialize in her rooms as well, she said, including a gray form that manifested by her bed that appeared to be watching the television she had positioned across the room. Once, according to her testimony, a presence seemed to sit atop her at night, making her unable to move. She was terrified and unable to move until the heaviness dissipated. Needless to say, she moved as soon as possible.

WHAT'S GOING ON AT THE SALINAS HIGH SCHOOL BELL TOWER?

Salinas High School is the oldest high school in the city and a striking fixture of the Salinas landscape. Founded in 1882, the school has been located on South Main Street in the heart of the Salinas community since 1920 and is part of four high schools that make up the Salinas Union High School District. In 1999, much of the campus was rebuilt, although the original bell tower and the main wing of the building were kept and subsequently renovated. More than 2,500 students were enrolled in the school during the 2016–17 school year, according to state records. Its notable alumni include author John Steinbeck, football players Joe Kapp and Evan Smith and Van Partible, creator of the *Johnny Bravo* cartoon, which aired on the Cartoon Network beginning in 1995.

Supernatural stories abound at the school and are particularly popular among the students, although there are faculty who have also claimed to witness supernatural events over the course of the school's long history. Disembodied voices have been heard in various locations, according to both students and staff. Often what they are saying and who the voices are calling to is a mystery. Sensors in the school cafeteria have also been activated by motion in the middle of the night, even though no physical cause could be determined for the activation.

One of the most prevalent stories of Salinas High School is the tale of a lovelorn girl who committed suicide on campus. According to the legend, this teen girl was overcome with grief after observing her boyfriend making out with another girl, which means you've been dumped in high school circles. Seeing no future for herself, she flung herself from the school's bell tower and fell to her death. According to the legend, students said they have been approached by a strange teenage girl who called herself Jennifer and asked if they knew her boyfriend named Adrian. According to these reports, the girl asked the students to tell him goodbye for her. The weird teen, they reported, was unknown to them and wasn't a student at the school so far as they knew. The girl would quickly vanish after making her request.

The bell tower is where many of the school's ghostly events are said to materialize. Janitors have claimed to hear odd sounds when they are cleaning in the vicinity of the tower, such as invisible footsteps, the sound of a crying girl and even the ringing of the bell in the dead of night. A photographer around 2014 allegedly captured a dark spirit on his camera

Pictured is the bell tower at Salinas High School, where it's said a teen girl once died after leaping to her death from the top. *Author's collection.*

when he took photos of the bell tower following a high school basketball game, although he didn't know it at the time. It was only when he posted the image to Instagram that some claimed to see the dark figure in the photo. It quickly went viral.

Current students have also reported strange sounds in other locations on campus. Two students said that they heard a pencil rolling down the aisles of the auditorium. The students looked to find the cause of the sound but found nothing. The rolling pencil continued to make noise, however, despite their fruitless search. While not a scary incident on its own, the feeling of something else in the room, a presence, caused the boys to quickly find another part of the school to hang out.

Salinas High School isn't the only high school in Salinas when it comes to ghostly encounters. One of the district's more popular stories concerns a white figure not just *seen* swimming in the pool at Alisal High School in 2009 but actually captured on a surveillance camera positioned over the pool. The security video of the phantasm was even posted to YouTube. In the grainy footage, a white blob of light is clearly visible making its way across the pool and back to the other side, as if a wisp of smoke were there practicing its breast stroke.

THE SPIRITS OF THE SALINAS CALIFORNIAN BUILDING

The *Salinas Californian* remains the oldest continuously published newspaper, not just in Monterey County but in the entire state of California. In 2021, the newspaper will celebrate its 150th year, which is quite a feat in this era of digital journalism. The *Californian* began as the *Salinas Index* on March 30, 1871. Its founder and editor, Melville Byerly, wrote that the sidewalks and streets (made for carriages at the time) needed improvements. To this day, the newspaper continues to report on the status of the community's roadways.

The *Index* transitioned to the *Salinas Californian* in 1942 under the leadership of publisher Paul H. Caswell. Caswell had become publisher in

The front entrance to the Salinas Californian Building in the downtown area. The newspaper has been a part of the community since 1871. *Author's collection.*

1939 and remained in that role until 1960. The newspaper quickly outgrew its original building due to the demand for more and more local coverage. The offices relocated to a newly constructed site at 123 Alisal Street in 1949. In its 1971 centennial edition, the newspaper proudly proclaimed that it never missed a single issue during the transition from one location to another. A panel over the building's main entrance offers visitors four carvings depicting the natural wealth found on the Central Coast to show their connection to the business landscape of Salinas: a head of lettuce for the Salinas Valley, horses for the ranching community, fish to signify Monterey Bay and press cylinders to symbolize the machines of industry and hard work found in the area.

While now owned by Gannet Company Inc., which bought the newspaper from Speidel Newspapers in 1977, the *Californian* continues to operate in the community to this day, although its staff levels have become less robust in recent years. Its offices moved to Main Street in 2017 due to an ever-shrinking demand for print newspapers. The presses, which once roared on Alisal Street, have gone silent as well, as the newspaper is now printed in San Jose and shipped back for local delivery. Over the years, the paper has covered a variety of big stories, from multiple-fatality vehicle crashes and the 1989 Loma Prieta Earthquake to its annual coverage of the famous Salinas Rodeo, which is an important tradition in the Valley.

This newspaper's long life, particularly at 123 Alisal Street, comes with a fair share of eerie encounters, as reported by employees working in the building. During the period when newspapers were shipped out of a landing bay on site, one manager reported that she often felt a presence looking over her shoulder, perhaps the spirit of a district manager who held the position years before she did, checking to ensure that she was doing a good job. In 2015, she also claimed to have seen a glimpse of a woman dressed in vintage clothing while in the building's downstairs restroom. The woman, she said, was simply applying lipstick and didn't seem to notice her. The presence of the ghostly woman in the bathroom could be attributed to an old rumor that, long ago, a woman fell down the stairs in the building and died as a result of the injuries she sustained in the accident.

Ghostly clatters have long been heard in the old building when it was in regular use. These include loud noises that revealed no cause upon investigation. What could be causing them? Two employees reported that they once heard a loud *thud* in another room but found no one in the room when they went in to see what caused the sound. Another reported that she

SALINAS CALIFORNIAN

YOUR
COUNTY SEAT
DAILY
NEWSPAPER

THE WEATHER

Consolidation Salinas Index-Journal, Established 1871 and Salinas Morning Post, Established 1933

NINETY-SECOND YEAR—NO. 224   SALINAS, CALIFORNIA, WEDNESDAY EVENING, SEPTEMBER 18, 1963   42 PAGES   THREE SECTIONS   10 CENTS

28 BRACEROS KILLED

Worst Bus Tragedy in State, U.S. History

71-Car Freight Shears Vehicle South of Chualar

(See Pictures, Page 22)

A Southern Pacific freight train sheared through a light-bodied labor bus at 65 miles-an-hour yesterday afternoon a mile south of Chualar and killed 28 Mexican national field workers.

The California highway patrol said today that the tragedy was "the biggest single fatal vehicle accident of any kind in the history of California." And the National Safety council labelled the previous "worst" accident, near Salt Lake City, Utah, when 26 persons perished.

Coroner Has Trouble Identifying Victims

Page 3, Col. 3

Farr Seeks State Probe Of Accident

WEARY, STUNNED, SORROWFUL

Eyewitness: 'All Those Guys Calling to Me . . .'

LOOK OUT BELOW

Today's Inside News

TODAY'S BASEBALL

MAN KILLED

SCENE OF IMPACT—Splintered bus bears mute witness to tragedy that claimed lives of many Mexican farm workers. The SP train, hauling 71 gondola and some box cars, was going about 65 miles an hour at time of crash, engineer said. Rescue teams can be seen along train checking dead. In background, at right, is U.S. 101.

WRECKAGE—Sheet metal side of Mexican national bus hangs across the front of the northbound Southern Pacific freight train, more than a mile from the point of impact. In background, a spectator looks at body caught beneath diesel engine (arrow). Train left dead strewn along tracks as it screeched to a stop. (Californian photo)

Rainstorm Boosts Salinas Above September's Average

Doctor Feels Quints Won't Suffer Ailment

The Salinas Californian often covers breaking news stories, such as the bus crash that killed twenty-eight people near Chualar outside Salinas in 1963. From the Salinas Californian.

heard the door knob rattle near her desk but found no one on the other side of the door when she investigated. The incident left her quite rattled. She refused to work alone in the building after that.

THE FLOATING SPIRIT OF STEINBECK HOUSE

John Steinbeck, one of America's most beloved authors, was born in Monterey County's agricultural hub, Salinas, in 1902, a town he would later immortalize in his award-winning novels. He wasn't born in a hospital, but rather in his home, a stately Victorian found on Central Avenue and reminiscent of the homes built in Pacific Grove. It was here where the author of such memorable tales as *East of Eden*, *The Grapes of Wrath* and *Of Mice and Men* played with his family and friends as a youngster. Steinbeck was the only boy in a home with three sisters. Here they also enjoyed the company of a pony, which he would later write about in the book *The Red Pony*, which was published in 1933.

The family's lovely Victorian quarters were built between 1897 and 1898. The Steinbecks moved into the home in 1900, two years before the author was born there. Steinbeck was born to John Ernst Steinbeck and Olive Hamilton Steinbeck. At the age of fourteen, he decided to become a writer, not realizing at the time that his decision would pay off. He would go on to earn both a Pulitzer and Nobel Prize. As an adult, Steinbeck returned with his wife, Carol, to help his father take care of Olive, who'd taken ill. While back in his childhood home, he penned two novels, *The Red Pony* and *Tortilla Flat*, the latter of which went on to become his first commercial success. When Olive died, the house was sold to new owners. Two subsequent families lived in the house following the Steinbecks, the last of which sold the home to the Catholic Diocese of Monterey. The home itself was used as both a boardinghouse and a clubhouse for students.

Today, Steinbeck House is owned by the Valley Guild, a nonprofit organization dedicated to maintaining the historic structure near the heart of the city for future generations of Steinbeck's fans. The guild began as the brainchild of a number of local women in 1973, many the wives of local Salinas growers. Their original goal was to open a restaurant featuring locally grown produce on the menu. The restaurant is currently operated by three

Author and Nobel Prize winner John Steinbeck, who was born in Salinas in 1902. *Photo by Olavi Kaskisuo/Lehtikuva.*

paid employees and a whopping eighty-four volunteers. Visitors come to the establishment from all fifty states and elsewhere around the world. In October 2018, Steinbeck aficionados from Poland, Belgium, Spain, England and Germany visited the former literary giant's home. Is it possible that Steinbeck still lives there?

Mysterious sightings are common at Steinbeck House. They include a number of unexplained phenomena, including a spectral character observed in the ornate downstairs front room, which some have attributed to Steinbeck himself making a house call. This strange presence has, at times, been observed shrouded in a mysterious yellow mist. In the ghost hunting world, these apparitions are referred to as "ectoplasm." Some simply refer to them as "ecto-mists." Similar to a vapor, these phantasms will often move around or simply hover in place. At times, the mists coalesce and form into a full ghost, although they can often simply vanish too. Ecto-mists are captured often on cameras by astute investigators.

Some claim to have seen a foggy, human-shaped form standing at the front window of the famous Steinbeck House. *Drawing by Paul Van de Carr.*

Other supernatural accounts come from a past Guild president, who reported her experience after working alone one night in the restaurant's kitchen. She said she turned around and found herself face to face with a strange, ethereal man. According to her account, the man vanished into thin air without so much as a single word. A chef at the restaurant reported a nearly identical experience in the same part of the kitchen, although the man's identity remains a mystery. Could it be Steinbeck, his father or someone else?

More recently, another odd confrontation with the unknown was reported in a different part of the home. A young mother brought her three-year-old boy to dine at the restaurant for what they hoped to be a fancy lunch. The two sat in what had been the Steinbecks' quaint living room. It was there the young boy reportedly stared at the ceiling, pointed upward and asked his mother, "What is that woman doing up there?" No one but the boy, however, could see anything. The two returned for lunch some weeks later, and the boy looked up and proclaimed, "She's still up there! What's she doing up there?" A volunteer at the home has indicated that this particular room is where Olive herself passed on after being sent home from the hospital following months of treatments for a series of strokes.

Phantasmic incidents at the Steinbeck House also include sounds and random electrical impulses, such as the vacuum cleaner turning on by itself and doors slamming on their own. These tales of hauntings have attracted ghost hunters of all calibers—thanks also to the Steinbeck name—some of whom indicated the presence of a young female spirit in the upstairs section of the house, the young girl thought to be nine or ten years old. One volunteer at the home said that Olive is likely the only person to have died in the home but added that an uncle may have also passed on there. There is no record of a small girl dying there, yet it is a girl that some have seen, next to the hazy form that likes to stand at the window.

THE CREEPINESS OF OLD STAGE ROAD

Old Stage Road is a long stretch of asphalt running along the eastern edge of the city, almost from the city's northern tip to its southern end. The stretch comes to an end at both San Juan Grade Road and Alisal Road. Over the

Old Stage Road in Salinas has left many with a nagging sense of fear. It's considered a hot spot for paranormal activity in the area. *Author's collection.*

years, the lonely stretch of asphalt along this agricultural community has played an integral role in a number of local legends.

The first is the old tale of the decapitated woman. According to the stories, of which there are many, a lone woman walked along the roadway and was offered a ride by a stranger on a carriage. Rather than take her to her destination, the stranger raped and murdered her. In fact, he decapitated her, the legend goes, and left her body to rot in a nearby field in a sloppy attempt to hide his heinous crime. To this day, the spirit of the woman is said to walk along Old Stage Road, holding her own head in her hands. While there are a number of people who live in the area today, a sense of dread can still be felt while driving along the roadway, according to locals who travel there regularly.

While no one knows the identity of the woman, most believe that she was murdered sometime in the late 1800s or early 1900s, during a time when there were fewer people residing in the area than can be found there now. There has been no official confirmation that a murder of that grim nature ever took place there, but the stories of the woman have remained constant despite a lack of supporting documentation.

Reports over the years have placed the headless apparition near an expanse of fields where the murders are alleged to have taken place. Others claimed that they've stopped on the road after seeing a woman dressed in white. Some have said they've given the strange woman a ride, only for her to vanish upon getting into the vehicle. One witness, who shared her experience on YouTube, claimed to have driven through a screaming female apparition along the road on Halloween night in 2005. When the vehicle came to a stop, the vehicle's occupants realized that the woman had vanished. The same witness, who shared her story online, reported that she later lived near the road and, in the dead of night, could still hear her distant screams some nights.

Some believe that the spirit of Old Stage Road may also be a spirit hailing from Japanese internment camps located in the area. Following the attack at Pearl Harbor on December 7, 1941, many Japanese and Japanese Americans were stripped of their possessions and forced to live in temporary camps. These camps were located throughout California before being closed in 1942, when the population was sent to larger internment camps. In Monterey County, more than 3,500 people were made to live in the temporary camps, which were called "Assembly Centers" at the time. While some say that the spirits could hail from this sad chapter in the county's history, others blame the Old Stage Road spirit on hangings that also occurred in the area during a more lawless period of Salinas's past.

The stories of hauntings along the roadway are so strong, in fact, that some claim that spirits, perhaps the woman of Old Stage Road herself, have wandered off to haunt nearby office buildings. Some have claimed that office workers in the area are often frustrated by odd, supernatural events, such as rearranged office supplies, radios that turn on and off and more. Other spirits may also haunt the roadway, as there have been multiple accounts of figures standing in the fields. These dark characters are seen at night, unmoving and not responding when drivers have stopped and called out to them. Can this be the woman of Old Stage Road and her killer or other restless spirits?

There are some who think that the headless woman of Old Stage Road, in all her dire incarnations, is a local spin on the legend of La Llorona, otherwise known as the Weeping Woman of the Southwest. According to the legend, the woman has long, flowing black hair, a heavenly face and one nasty disposition. It's commonly believed that she drags screaming children away from their families with the sole intent to drown them in chilly lakes and rivers. Others claim that she is a woman by the name of Maria who mourns the loss of her two beautiful children who drowned. There are still others who believe that La Llorona drowned her own children in the futile hope that she might have more time for the suitors courting her. Most think her to be a terrible, malicious spirit with murder on her mind.

Whether Maria or not, the headless woman of Old Stage Road has created a legend all her own—one that warns drivers not to pick up strange women they find along that particular road, unless they want their passenger to disappear shortly after she's climbed into the car.

Los Coches Adobe

While Stokes Adobe may be considered one of Monterey's most haunted locales, it is Los Coches Adobe that takes the prize in Monterey County's southern reaches. It's possible, in fact, that Los Coches Adobe is the scariest and most haunted of Monterey County's otherworldly landmarks, due to the sense of sheer terror the spot has left in the minds of some who have visited there. Located in the Soledad community, between Greenfield and King City, the former rooming house and stagecoach stop still stands, although it's boarded up and fenced off to keep visitors from entering the dark property. Today, the land appears dismal and neglected, covered in overgrown grass and weeds; the two-story building's windows are boarded shut with rotting planks. There is a feeling of dread that creeps over you as you get closer to the main entrance of the adobe. Most, however, simply zip past as they sit comfortably in their vehicles. The alleged haunted property is a stone's throw from Highway 101. Vehicles speed by every few seconds, most never knowing how close they've come to one of the area's creepiest ghostly hot spots. Most never even notice the old place.

In English, Los Coches Adobe roughly translates into "the Car Adobe." It's a fitting name for the property, for it did eventually become a stagecoach stop for travelers to San Francisco and Los Angeles, albeit one with a dark history. It's also commonly believed that the large structure was once a brothel, attracting a large number of miners and businessmen passing through town.

Built in 1843, the Soberanes rancho was the property of Maria Josefa Soberanes. It sat on nearly nine thousand acres of land, given in the memory of Josefa's father, Jose Soberanes, two years earlier from Mexican governor Juan Alvarado. It's located within an easy hike to the Mission Soledad. Josefa built a two-room adobe on the land with her husband, William Brunner Richardson. The small home was soon made larger, however, when the family converted the home into a more pronounced two-story structure. After a series of financial misfortunes, the family, faced with losing their cherished Soledad rancho, was forced to open their home to visitors in order to make ends meet. It became a stopping point for stagecoach travelers making their way north and south in the mid- to late 1800s. More nefarious deeds are also rumored to have occurred there, including the rancho's use as a brothel, as well as multiple murders. Josefa, it is alleged, killed a number of travelers fresh from mining camps located in the Sierra Mountains. It's said that after committing her heinous acts, Josefa tossed the bodies of her victims into a nearby well before hiding their valuables on the property. This has led to the rumor that besides the ghosts of the dead, a treasure can also be found on the Los Coches Adobe property. Famed outlaws Three-Fingered Jack and Joaquin Murrieta are also believed by some to have aided in the murders. They are also thought to be among the spirits haunting the property, although neither died there. More than thirty miners are also believed to have died in a nearby mining accident, leading to what some call a heavy spiritual presence on the property.

The rancho remained a popular stop into the 1870s, when the Southern Pacific Railroad came through. Accommodations for those jumping from train to stagecoach remained a need in the area, even after the land became the property of David Jacks, who also owned property in the Monterey area closer to the sea. About a century later, his daughter, Margaret Jacks, donated the adobe, along with ten acres of land, to the State of California.

Over the years, visitors to the area have reported strange, disembodied voices on the property and coming from within the building. A lady in black, perhaps Josefa herself, has been seen moving about the building. The apparition has also reportedly been seen around the well into which it is believed the victims were thrown. A female voice has also been heard around the building even though no one was observed there at the time.

Screams have also been heard on the property, often from the well, according to some accounts. Others have reported cold spots, which they attribute to the woman in black, and other stories depict spirits acting aggressively, tugging and pushing anyone who makes their way through the old rancho. Some have also reported a negative energy in the structure, one so potent it has created a "bad mood" in the person after they walked inside the building. Other encounters have included sightings of shadowy figures, a "force" that throws people to the ground, the spirit of a man with shattered teeth, a man in black and another figure hanging by his neck from the branches of a tree near the adobe. Others have reported seeing the wandering ghosts of men in prison attire, thought to be deceased inmates from the nearby prison in Soledad. There are so many reports, many found via a simple Google search, that one has to wonder exactly what dark energies are stored there.

The sordid history of Los Coches Adobe has attracted national attention as well. It was featured on an episode of the hit television show *Ghost Adventures* in 2015, which featured the haunted location in its tenth season. Paranormal investigators are often drawn there due to the dark energies some believe can be found there. One particular researcher, who claims to have seen the ghost of the woman in black, refuses to return to the property. Whether one believes the supernatural tales, the property itself has historical value. As of 2019, efforts have been underway to restore the site to its original state, although those that haunt the place likely will not be affected one way or another. Their presence will remain for eternity.

A Rest Stop Encounter Outside King City

Rest stops, in general, aren't the kind of places that spring to mind when thinking about the unknown. Like anywhere, however, they too can be a hot spot for spiritual encounters. For one couple returning to the Salinas area from Los Angeles, their midnight stop at a local rest area came with a helping of the supernatural.

While once quite common in the United States, rest stops were once a mecca for travelers. They don't just offer bathroom opportunities—they offer grassy areas for people and pets, as well as vending machines and picnic tables for families to rest before piling, once more, into the family vehicle. While some rest areas offer basic amenities, such as water fountains and toilets, the flashier ones are staffed with tourist information personnel and cleaning staff.

Today, rest areas are quickly becoming a thing of the past, being replaced by travel plazas that offer one-stop shopping, not to mention high-tech bathrooms. In these locations, travelers get more than a quick break; they get restaurants, gasoline and maybe even a hot cup of strong coffee. Many states have closed their rest areas as a result of slower traffic and due to budget costs in state transportation departments, which are tasked with running the rest stops.

They haven't been around all that long, but since their inception in 1956 with the United States Interstate Highway, rest areas quickly became a part of the American landscape. By design these stops were often constructed in desolate areas where there were long stretches of road with little to no amenities. These days, amenities are found in abundance, decreasing the need for rest areas, although many still exist, with some in California located along Highway 101.

While rest stops aren't commonly thought to be spooky places, one such rest area outside King City may change your mind. *Author's collection.*

The couple driving home to Salinas pulled into a particular rest area found outside King City for a quick trip to the bathroom, little realizing that their stop would bring them face to face with the supernatural. According to the woman, her husband pulled into the stop and faced the women's restroom. Her husband went first and then waited for the woman near their vehicle. Upon leaving the bathroom, the woman reported that she very nearly ran right into a strange man outside. While she couldn't see his face, the man appeared to be a rancher or cowboy, as he wore denim jeans, a cowboy hat and even cowboy boots. Although startled, the woman reported the stranger to be good natured. He even said, "Good evening" to her. When she told her husband, who was nearby waiting for her, how the man startled her, her husband became anxious. No one had been near her, according to him. He told her that he'd kept his eyes on her the entire time as she was walking toward him and there hadn't been a soul around. He said she did pause for a moment, as though she had been scared, but there had been no one around.

The ghosts of deceased cowboys are a theme in the area, according to stories shared by locals. One such incident happened recently. A man was driving under an old bridge in King City when he saw a vehicle pulled off to the right shoulder. Skids marks were visible behind the car, indicating that it had slammed on the brakes when it stopped. As the man noticed this, a cowboy appeared right in front of his vehicle, causing him to slam on his brakes as well. The man was described as wearing denim jeans, tan boots and a cowboy hat, all quite similar to the cowboy seen in the middle of the night at the rest stop. After his abrupt stop, the man reportedly looked for the cowboy and realized that he was nowhere in sight. The cowboy had mysteriously vanished. At that time, the car behind him got back on the roadway, and both vehicles, with slightly bewildered drivers behind the wheels, continued on their way.

Tales of the mysterious cowboy, perhaps the same cowboy at both the rest stop and under the bridge, have been shared in the community since the 1980s, according to some. Many believe that it's the spirit of a drunk driver who perished in a crash after being ejected from the front window of his vehicle. It's their belief that this spirit is still wandering, trying to decipher what happened in those final moments of life.

It isn't surprising that King City would be home to more western-themed spirits. Where there are ranches, cowboys (and their ghosts) are never far behind. Named for Charles King and made famous by John Ernst Steinbeck, father of author John Steinbeck, who claimed to be King City's first resident, the area is well known for its agricultural contributions and ranches found throughout the area. Originally, the land was nicknamed the "great Salinas desert," according to the city's history page. King, however, saw the potential in the land thanks to its closeness to the wild Salinas River and quickly became successful in the wheat trade. By the late 1800s, the city had become a thriving city for those looking to work the land.

THE MYSTERIOUS STROLLER OF MOSS LANDING AND CASTROVILLE

Located along Highway 1 between Marina and Watsonville, the Moss Landing community is an interesting member of the Central Coast community, not just because of tales of ghostly phenomena, but for other reasons as well. While there aren't as many full-time residents in the coastal fishing community as there are living in other Monterey County communities, Moss Landing provides a quaint village-like atmosphere to those who do call the area home. Mixed with that are the tourists who stop there on their way north and south to either Santa Cruz or Monterey. It's a popular spot for visitors thanks to its whale watching and kayaking opportunities. Wildlife can also be found in abundance there, particularly sea birds, seals and otters, one of the favorite sights for visitors to Monterey Bay.

Elkhorn Slough Reserve is also located in Moss Landing and is an area frequented by visitors locally and abroad for its natural beauty and hiking trails. Besides being at the head of Elkhorn Slough, Moss Landing also boasts a prime location at the head of the underwater abyss known as Monterey Canyon. The area is home to research vessels and scientists with the Monterey Bay Aquarium Research Institute and other marine laboratories. One of the more striking features, courtesy of the Moss Landing Power Plant, is the double smoke stacks visible from both ends of the Monterey Peninsula, from Pacific Grove to Santa Cruz. Not even the big quake of 1989 toppled them, even though it did destroy other structures nearby.

Its attraction as a fishing port has brought many to the community over the years, and some have decided not to leave, even after death. One such spirit is said to haunt a popular inn along Moss Landing Road.

This photo from the mid-1960s shows the harbor area at Moss Landing, where, nearby, a strange woman has been seen walking in the night. *California State University–Monterey Bay.*

The site was formerly a mansion and then offices with quarters located upstairs; author Jeff Dwyer has reported the spirit of a young girl in the upstairs area.

Hemingway may have written *The Old Man and the Sea*, but the Old Man of the Sea was once thought to live just outside of Moss Landing's foggy cove, another claim to fame for the small community. Named "Bobo" for short, the creature was believed to have a bill similar to a duck and a head the size of a fifty-gallon barrel. It was first seen in the early 1900s by Captain Sal Colletto as he piloted his salmon fishing vessel off the shore of Santa Cruz. At the time, he pulled alongside the creature thinking at first it was a human floating in the sea. He soon realized that it was a creature of some kind and fled the scene. That wasn't the last he would see of the strange creature, however. Sixteen long years later, Colletto again found himself in a boat coming up alongside the creature. It looked worn and haggard those many years later, according to his account, with eyes that looked like grapefruit and a long, wrinkled brown body. Soon others claimed to have laid eyes on the creature off Moss Landing. He was quickly nicknamed Bobo, the Old Man of the Sea, although sightings of the creature were quite rare from that point forward.

Bobo is thought to have perished, as a matter of fact, in the year 1925, when a body matching the sea creature's description washed up on the shore two miles north of Santa Cruz. While terribly decomposed and hard to identify, scholars didn't believe that the odd-shaped body belonged to a whale or large shark. One scientist, E.L. Wallace, pondered that the remains could very well have belonged to a plesiosaurus, a creature left over from the planet's Jurassic period, and wondered whether a pocket of the creatures survived within the Monterey submarine canyon, which abuts Moss Landing's beach. While his theory might have been true, no such creature was ever reported again.

While not a haunting, the mysterious Bobo is one of the facets of Moss Landing's storied past that makes the area an attraction for visitors.

It's said, however, that the ghostly presence of an adult woman walks the residential streets of Moss Landing when the sun has set and the moon has risen. No one knows the identity of the mysterious stroller in the dark. The woman seemingly vanishes into the mist, only to reappear again just as she was on other nights.

Just a short drive from Moss Landing's beautiful inlet is the city of Castroville, known as the artichoke center of the world, a fact made more famous by actress Marilyn Monroe when she was named honorary Artichoke Queen in 1948. Only it isn't Marilyn that haunts the streets in and around the community. Like Moss Landing, a wandering woman has also been reported by locals. Could it be the same woman as the one wandering a few miles away closer to Elkhorn Slough? The woman is thought to be wearing a simple dress, though one with a distinctly vintage design. Like the young girl in the inn, this woman's identity remains a mystery.

On one occasion, a motorist reported a woman blocking the roadway, not allowing their vehicle (heading to the Casa De Campo area) to pass. The woman stared directly into the vehicle, according to witnesses, and never made an attempt to get out of the way. She was so close that they could see she was not wearing any shoes, but was walking barefoot on the road. Oddly enough, she vanished seconds later, leaving a very bewildered set of witnesses behind. A woman matching this description has been seen in other neighborhoods as well, usually wandering the streets in the dead of night, including 4:00 a.m. in one instance. In this report, the mysterious woman looked to be limping along the roadway. On other occasions, some have claimed to see the lone woman walking with what appeared to be a very large dog.

Prunedale is a small community located on the outskirts of Monterey County, near both Salinas and Moss Landing. The area is rural and sits at a modest elevation of ninety-two feet above sea level. The community is believed to have been founded by Charles Langley, a banker from nearby Watsonville. He operated the first Prunedale Post Office, which closed in 1908 only to reopen nearly fifty years later in 1953. A plum orchard was once located where the community sits today, although a lack of fertilizer and proper irrigation made the endeavor short-lived. The name Prunedale, however, stuck.

The town grew over the years, particularly following the construction of Highway 101 through the community. The highway was built there between 1931 and 1932. Today, there are more than seventeen thousand people living in the community. As Prunedale grew, so did the number of eerie encounters.

It's in Prunedale where one family encountered three spirits that might have dated back to the community's founding. Their supernatural encounter occurred in 1992, shortly after they moved into an old home on McGuffie Road thought to be built in the 1920s. The property backs up to Manzanita County Park. The quaint home was like any other, but empty, as the couple had not yet moved all the way in. Tired after a long day of moving, the two decided to call it a day. They decided rather than move in the mattress, erect the bedframe and dress the bed, they would simply make do by sleeping on the floor in the living room in front of their comfortable fireplace. After throwing together a makeshift bed, they settled in for the night.

While her husband slept, the woman said she had a harder time dozing off right away. Movement then brought her wide awake. According to her report, shapes were making their way through the house from the area of the home's older kitchen. When she sat up to see what the movement was, she saw three young children as clear as day, two girls and one young boy, all aged between six and ten. All three, she said, were dressed in old sleeping gowns of the sort one might imagine Ebenezer Scrooge wearing in *A Christmas Carol*. The boy wore a simple nightshirt, while the two girls' sleeping gowns were adorned with ruffles at the ends of the sleeves.

The three children, according to the woman's testimony, meandered slowly from the kitchen and walked right through a wall, disappearing into the neighboring bedroom. The woman closed her eyes, uttering a silent prayer for the children to find peace in the afterlife. Throughout the encounter, she said she never felt an ounce of fear. But her encounter wasn't over.

After making her silent prayer, the woman opened her eyes again when she felt a presence in the room. The young boy, she said, stood mere inches from her. The two locked eyes for the briefest moment in astonishment. When she jumped in surprise, so did the young spirit, who subsequently vanished. She never saw the three children again and said that the encounter didn't prevent her from living in the comfortable old home for many years.

BIG SUR: A LIGHTHOUSE AND DARKER BEINGS

Big Sur encompasses a wild, winding section of Highway 1 south of Carmel and north of the infamous Hearst Castle. It can be a long, lonely stretch of road at times, blanketed in fog and chilling cliffs. At other times, it's teeming with tourists, buses, bicyclists and road construction crews. The Santa Lucia Mountains rise majestically to the east, with the deep waters of the Pacific Ocean spreading out in all its glory to the west. Full of wilderness, wildlife, resorts, restaurants and beautiful residences, Big Sur is home to the world-famous Nepenthe's Restaurant and the Esalen Institute and has been home to an assortment of celebrities over the year, most notably the author Henry Miller, the once-famous Bobby Darin and plenty more. Authors Jack Kerouac and Hunter S. Thompson are also among those who've stayed in the cool shadows of the Big Sur forest.

Once called El Sur Grande, Big Sur is estimated to encompass ninety miles. It's both treacherous and scenic, particularly for early settlers to the area. Highway 1 was not completed until 1937, and this brought a measure of civilization to the community of loggers and those seeking a life of solitude. Until that time, residents depended on the Old Coast Trail to make their way in and out of the community. Ships would dock there as well and

Point Sur Lighthouse near Big Sur, south of Carmel, is the site of a number of reported incidents involving unexplained phenomena. *Presidio of Monterey.*

were guided safely to their destination thanks to the Point Sur Lighthouse Station, built in 1889.

Four light keepers and their families operated the lighthouse twenty-four hours a day. Every four months, a ship bearing supplies would attend to the remote outpost. There the families received food, coal, wood for fires and feed for their animals from a whaling skiff sent from an anchored delivery vessel. Despite the beacon of light warning seafarers of the craggy California shoreline, a number of vessels met their demise near Point Sur. Many believe that those who died in the shipwrecks can be seen around the lighthouse to this day, drawn to the light as a moth is drawn to flame. Many who drowned likely saw the shining light as they struggled in the deadly tide. A tall man dressed in navy blue nineteenth-century clothing has been observed there on numerous occasions, wandering forlornly around the property. Could he be a sailor lost to those same deadly waters found right offshore? Cold spots have also been attributed to the apparition. These treacherous waters took to the depths a number of vessels over the years, including the *Ventura*, lost in 1875 before construction of the lighthouse. Others sank despite the lighthouse, including the *Los Angeles* in 1894, the *Majestic* in 1909 and the *Shna-Yak* in 1916, among others. The *Howard Olson* sank more recently in 1956. Besides ships, an airship also met its end in the seas near the lighthouse. The navy's USS *Macon* crashed into the depths on February 12, 1935, with a loss of eighty-one crew members. Two survived. Searchers with the Monterey Bay Aquarium Research Institute and the U.S. Navy discovered the wreckage of the helium-filled dirigible, which measured 785 feet in length, in 1990.

Now known as the Point Sur State Historic Park, tours are led on the lighthouse property, including night tours for those looking to spot a sailor out of time and out of body. Recovered pieces of the *Macon's* wreckage have also been put on display for those seeking to glimpse a relic of historical disaster.

The lighthouse is also thought to be the home of another spirit, that of an eighteen-year-old young woman who died in the early 1900s from tuberculosis in the living quarters. The young lady lived on the upper floor and could often be heard coughing during her last weeks of life. When she eventually passed away there, the sound of her coughing continued. In fact, reports of the sound of a coughing woman continue to this day, from the same room where the young lady died.

The lighthouse is so haunted, in fact, that it's listed as one of the top ten most haunted lighthouses in America.

Farther into the wilderness, where the shore turns to damp, shadowy forest, many have claimed to witness a different sort of supernatural occurrence. Over the years, beings of shadow and mystery have been spotted in the Big Sur wilderness. These creatures, having been witnessed so often, have come to be called the Dark Watchers. Although their name may connote sinister intent, most believe the Dark Watchers to be benevolent. And while many agree that the watchers have long been a part of the community, some claim that they are tall and thin beings made of shadow and wind. Many others have claimed that they are small, going so far as to nickname them "the little people." Others claim not to have seen them but to have felt a definite presence, of unseen eyes, watching from the shadows of the forest.

Reports of the Dark Watchers are legion. They've been discussed at length among Big Sur residents and even indigenous peoples, Spaniards and Mexicans when the region was far more wild than it is today. These watchers have been seen primarily when the sun is making its rounds, either at dusk or dawn, at a time when shadows stretch long across the landscape. There are those who believe them to be aliens, creatures from another world who crashed in the Santa Lucia Mountains long ago. Other believe them to be more earthbound, ancient beings that have largely managed to avoid human encounters over the years. Oddly enough, Big Sur isn't their only home. Reports of encounters with the Dark Watchers range from San Luis Obispo to the north of Monterey

Artist's rendering of the watchers of Big Sur, which many have claimed to have seen over the years. *Drawing by Paul Van de Carr.*

County in the Santa Cruz Mountains. Authors have written about these strange beings on numerous occasions as well. Tor House poet Robinson Jeffers wrote of them in his poem "Such Counsels You Gave to Me."

John Steinbeck has referred to the watchers in his writing, advising, as others have, that it is best to simply ignore them and go about your business. It's also rumored that Steinbeck's mother, Olive, while teaching in the area in the late 1800s, had numerous encounters with beings she described as roughly three feet tall. Steinbeck's own son, Thomas, has written about them as well, and even scientist Ed Ricketts, whom we met in an earlier chapter, claimed to see them. Local ghost writer Randall A. Reinstedt, to whom this book is dedicated, has written about a number of the tales attributed to these creatures as well. Still others have claimed to see a figure in Big Sur's Santa Lucia Mountains that may or may not be connected to the mysterious watchers. Two sightings were reported of a dark figure in what appeared to be a long black coat, or perhaps a cloak, with a face obscured by darkness. In the first sighting, the gloomy figure was observed standing on a bluff but quickly vanished from sight. The next sighting offered a more detailed description of the black-clad figure, however. According to the witness, a policeman on a hunting expedition in the rugged countryside, he observed a terrifying face, largely obscured with coverings over much of his lower face and a hat atop his head. His eyes, according to the report, were simply not there. Despite this, he stared right at the policeman, only to vanish a moment later, much to the shock of the shaken officer.

Another more recent tale of Big Sur takes place in Pfeiffer State Beach. The day-use beach, while not open at night, is one of Big Sur's more popular tourist destinations. Here a ten-year-old girl drowned in the late 1990s, with both her mother and her grandmother also drowning in an attempt to rescue her. The family, who was visiting the coast for the Big Sur Marathon, hailed from Kansas. According to a *New York Times* article on the incident, Ivy was swept out to sea after getting caught in the surf near Point Sur. All three family members were pulled from the ocean, although Ivy's grandmother was pronounced dead at the scene. Her mother, and Ivy herself, later died at the hospital. To this day, sightings of a young girl matching her description have been reported on the beaches in the area.

In one such case, a young woman visiting Pfeiffer Beach said that she observed a small girl playing in the surf and grew concerned about her safety, as the young girl appeared to be all alone. The observer was distracted by a companion for only a moment, but when she turned back to say something to the girl, she was nowhere to be found. Others have reported near identical incidents and have identified the girl as having brown hair, a white shirt and dark shorts. Residents believe that Ivy, while not a local by birth, is now a part of the Big Sur coastline.

Other strange tales concern Highway 1, which runs through Big Sur on its way south to Cambria and Morro Bay. While there have been many strange sightings along the winding roadway, from mysterious objects in the sky to odd lights at sea, others have seen supernatural phenomena on the road itself.

One such incident occurred in the late 1980s as two men were driving north on Highway 1 toward Carmel two hours before midnight. The two observed lights in the distance ahead but simply thought, as most people would, that the lights were coming from an oncoming vehicle. As they drew closer, however, they realized that the lights were from something far stranger. According to one of the men, who recounted his story to Reinstedt, they came upon a man with flowing white hair and a long white beard. He was dressed in what appeared to be a monk's habit, holding a long wooden staff and wearing sandals. The oddest part of the encounter, however, was that the old man seemed to be emanating light. The two men continued past the glowing "wizard," and they lost sight of him when their car went around a bend in the road. To this day, no one knows for certain who the glowing magician was or what he was doing on the highway.

Another strange tale concerns that of a ghostly biplane thought to haunt Bixby Canyon, home of the world-famous Bixby Bridge. The World War I–era plane flies from the sea, under the bridge and up into the canyon, where it disappears. Many claim that they can hear the vintage plane at night, making its ghostly pass under the bridge over and over again. Stay the night in the canyon and you may hear the sound of the ghostly biplane yourself.

Add these to the oddly hypnotizing images of ghosts caught on camera that have been shared online, which includes a 2006 photo that shows a detailed and dramatic white haze appearing over a hand rail with a large tree in the background. Could the haze be the phantasmic remains of one of Big Sur's former residents? Another photograph shows two men posing humorously for the camera with their feet atop a stone and their hands on their chin. Surrounding them are a flurry of smoky shapes, glowing forms and what some believe are spirit orbs. The two men, too busy posing, are oblivious to the supernatural elements.

Could these spirits be amused by the two men? Could it be a dirty lens on the camera? No one may ever really know the answer, or the truth, but the haunts continue. Tales of ghostly encounters will remain a part of our very human history.

BIBLIOGRAPHY

Atlas Obscura. "Monterey's Custom House." www.atlasobscura.com.

———. "Old Monterey Jail." www.atlasobscura.com.

California Beaches. "These 13 Haunted Places by the California Coast Will Creep You Out." www.californiabeaches.com.

California Department of Parks and Recreation. "Old Whaling Station." www.parks.ca.gov.

California Paranormal Research. "Private Residence, Monterey Rd., Seaside, CA (Fort Ord)." http://phcal.com.

Cannery Row. "A History that's Unforgettable." https://canneryrow.com.

Carmel Pine Cone. "Ghost Hunters Search Tor House for Jeffers, Find His Wife Instead." www.pineconearchive.com.

City of Monterey Museums. "Monterey History." www.monterey.org.

City of Soledad, California. "Los Coches Adobe." https://cityofsoledad.com.

Dwyer, Jeff. *Ghost Hunter's Guide to Monterey and California's Central Coast*. Gretna, LA: Pelican Publishing Company, 2010.

Ghost Adventures. "Los Coches Adobe." The Travel Channel. www.travelchannel.com.

Ghosts and Gravestones. "5 Most Common Types of Ghosts and Spirits." www.ghostsandgravestones.com.

Ghosts of America. "Ghost Sightings." http://www.ghostsofamerica.com.

Haunted Houses. "Stevenson House." www.hauntedhouses.com.

Haunted Places. "Haunted Places in Monterey County, California." www. hauntedplaces.org.

Karman, James. *Robinson Jeffers, Poet of California*. N.p., 1987.

KSBW 8. "Ghost Hunting from Monterey to Big Sur." www.ksbw.com.

Lowman, Robert P. *Mission San Carlos Borromeo*. Arroyo Grande, CA: Lowman Publishing Company, 2013.

Mercury News. "Ghosts with the Most in Old Monterey." www.mercurynews. com.

———. "Historic California Posts, Camps, Stations and Airfields, Fort Ord (Camp Gigling, Camp Ord, Camp Clayton)." The California State Military Museum. http://www.militarymuseum.org.

Monterey Bay Parent. "Looking for Ghosts in Monterey County?" http:// www.montereybayparent.com.

Monterey County Historical Society. "King City, Monterey County, California." http://mchsmuseum.com.

———. "A Short History of Salinas, California." http://mchsmuseum. com.

Monterey County Weekly. "Big Sur Is Home to Shadowy Figures—or at Least People Who See Them." www.montereycountyweekly.com.

———. "The Tale of Bobo, Monterey Bay's Sea Creature, Resurfaces." http://www.montereycountyweekly.com.

Monterey: Grab Life by the Moments. "Hauntings & Ghost Stories of Monterey #1: "The Lady in Lace." www.seemonterey.com.

———. "Hauntings & Ghost Stories of Monterey #2: The Ghost at Robert Louis Stevenson House." www.seemonterey.com.

Moss Landing Marine Laboratories. "History of MLML." www.mlml. calstate.edu.

New York Times. "3 Members of a Family Drown in Sea at Big Sur." www. nytimes.com.

Reinstedt, Randall A. *Ghostly Tales and Mysterious Happenings of Old Monterey*. Monterey, CA: Ghost Town Publications, 1977.

———. *Ghosts, Bandits & Legends of Old Monterey, Carmel, and Surrounding Areas*. Monterey, CA: Ghost Town Publications, 1975, 1995.

———. *Ghosts of the Big Sur Coast*. Monterey, CA: Ghost Town Publications, 2002.

———. *Incredible Ghosts of Old Monterey's Hotel Del Monte*. Monterey, CA: Ghost Town Publications, 1980.

Salinas Californian. "Ghostly Encounters Spook Residents." www. thecalifornian.com.

————. "Spooky Sightings in Eerie Salinas." www.thecalifornian.com.

Seavey, Kent, and the Heritage Society of Pacific Grove. *Pacific Grove*. Charleston, SC: Arcadia Publishing, 2005.

SFGATE. "Ghost Hunting in Historic Monterey." www.sfgate.com.

Spookadar "Custom House." https://spookadar.com.

Steinbeck, John. *The Pearl*. London: Penguin Books, 2002.

USA Today. "Why Old-Fashioned Highway Rest Stops Are Disappearing." www.usatoday.com.

Yasuda, Anita. *Haunted Monterey Peninsula*. Atglen, PA: Schiffer Publishing Ltd., 2009.

Your Ghost Stories. "The Haunted Office." www.yourghoststories.com.

ABOUT THE AUTHOR

Patrick Whitehurst is a fiction and nonfiction author who has written three books for the Arcadia Publishing Images of America series. As a journalist, he produced content for a number of newspapers, covering everything from the heartbreaking deaths of nineteen Granite Mountain Hotshots to President Barack Obama's visit to Grand Canyon. He's also the author of the novellas *Monterey Noir* and *Monterey Pulp*, with a third, *Monterey Lies*, in the works. His most recent book, *The Pacific Grove Museum of Natural History*, was published in the Images of America series in 2018. The book covers the story behind the beloved Pacific Grove landmark and features the historical stories behind many of the museum's treasured collection items. He's also written the book *Williams*, which covers the history of a small town in northern Arizona, and the book *Grand Canyon's Tusayan Village*, on the history of the community at the entrance to the massive national park. He lives with his fiancée and four little dogs in Tucson, Arizona. Whitehurst was born and raised on the Central Coast, with his second hometown located near Flagstaff in the pine forest of northern Arizona. In the process of writing *Haunted Monterey County*, he visited nearly every site covered in the book but still has not seen a ghost himself.

Visit him online at patrickwhitehurst.com.